## Using Imagination to Explore
# The Dawn of Man

"Why must humanity and its history necessarily be young? Why this limitation, instead of the idea of perpetual recurrence, the eternity of man? Is there any proof that any cultures are irrevocably mortal? We know far too few of them to establish a law. There are cultures that apparently flowered for thousands of years. Some of the cultures that we call primitive have already existed for so long that they seem to have no beginning and no end. Are they immortal then? Might not the truth be that during past ages man has often tried to climb the rungs of the ladder that lead to a high immortal culture, but has slipped and fallen? Perhaps we are even now in the process of building a culture that will know immortality on earth and in heaven. This optimistic theory will bring a tired smile to many people's lips, for today a cynical doom-ridden attitude is the fashion. But . . . during the days when we were writing this book, challenging forward-looking slogans like these appeared on the walls of the Sorbonne: 'Professors, you are turning us into old people' and 'All power to imagination!' There's something that speaks out loud and clear against the tired smile!" *(From the Introduction)*

**Other Avon Books by
Louis Pauwels and Jacques Bergier**

THE MORNING OF THE MAGICIANS
IMPOSSIBLE POSSIBILITIES

# THE ETERNAL MAN

## LOUIS PAUWELS
## JACQUES BERGIER

*Translated by*

Michael Heron

AVON
PUBLISHERS OF BARD, CAMELOT, DISCUS, EQUINOX AND FLARE BOOKS

AVON BOOKS
A division of
The Hearst Corporation
959 Eighth Avenue
New York, New York 10019

First Avon Printing, September, 1973.

AVON TRADEMARK REG. U.S. PAT. OFF. AND
FOREIGN COUNTRIES, REGISTERED TRADEMARK—
MARCA REGISTRADA, HECHO EN CHICAGO, U.S.A.

Printed in the U.S.A.

# Contents

# Illustrations

(*Between pages* 128 *and* 129)

Do the facial features of this angel from Reims Cathedral, from the second century A.D., already show the promise of a rising civilization?

Les penseurs (the thinkers).

Who's Who?

They came in order to show themselves to the white men and to each other.

There is no explanation for his isolation, nor for the stagnation in his technological and cultural development. The king worships in service of the godhead with the lion shoulders. This is narrated by an inscription in Yazilikaya, in the Hurrite language.

The most famous masterpiece from the middle kingdom: The procession of Yazilikaya, cut out in the rocks.

Two sphynxes are still standing guard on the ruins of the capital of the Hethites, now the Turkish village of Aladja Höyük.

The Hethites were true masters of expressive art in the East.

Facial expression and dagger are reminiscent of another mysterious people, that of Luristan in Western Persia.

(Louvre, Paris) Sa-oud, king of Uruk, grandson of Lugalkisalsi.

(Louvre, Paris) About 1500 B.C. the worshipper illustrated here lived in Mesopotamia.

Hieroglyphs—Easter Island (Ethnographic Museum, Paris). Perhaps the moment is near for us to discover that systematic signals are being sent through space and that somewhere in the Great Ring of Intelligence in the universe telegraphists are busy sending out interstellar telegrams . . .

# THE ETERNAL MAN

# Introduction

Our culture wears blinkers, like all other cultures. A host of minor gods, who are only powerful because we agree not to question their validity, distract our attention from the fantastic aspect of reality. The blinkers limit our vision. We do not realize that there is another world within our world, that there is another man inside the man we ourselves are. Man must break his mental shackles, become a barbarian again. And first and foremost he must be a realist, i.e. he must proceed from the principle that reality is an unknown. If we made full use of all the knowledge at our disposal; if we established unsuspected connections between the various branches of knowledge; if we looked the facts in the face without prejudice; if we behaved towards knowledge like a foreigner who does not know the rules in force and simply tries to understand, we should constantly be discovering the fantastic side by side with what we call reality.

Basically, this is science's way of looking at things, provided we understand by science not merely what nineteenth century academic tradition has made out of it under the cloak of rationalism, but everything that our intellect can range over, without despising the unusual, without excluding what does not seem to fit into the accepted mold. We cannot foresee exactly what form knowledge will take later, nor whether it will be based on concepts that we neglect today and whose importance will only be discovered by our descendants.

The mind is like a parachute; it only functions when it is open. The authors' sole aim in writing this book is to induce men to keep their minds as open as possible so that they may win insights into the fields of knowledge previously hidden by their blinkers. Then the man with an open mind will find himself transported into a world that is just as wonderful, intricate and vast as that of the physicist, the astronomer or the mathematician. Fortunately, there is continuity. Man, his past, his future—they all conceal complicated mysteries, tell of the infinite, sing the music of the spheres. Anyone who despairs or feels bored in the midst of the countless wonders and enigmas that surround us must have an ignorant heart, a loveless intelligence. "Oh, the world is so beautiful", Paul Claudel makes one of his heroes cry, "that someone ought to live here who never has need of sleep!"

Of course, the road to the recognition of miracles and the solving of puzzles is not free of danger. We have to put forward a lot of daring hypotheses and traverse a desert of illusions and mirages before we arrive at one new truth. Yet it can happen that some really useful and valid piece of knowledge is produced from dubious premises.

One of my friends, a manufacturer of perfume essences, practices his profession on a large estate in the South of France. These essences are the highly concentrated extract of flowers and are used in the composition of different perfumes. As my friend is both imaginative and hospitable, he had laid out a park for his visitors, the walks in which consist of carpets of flowers, which they crush as they walk down them. This sends up exquisite waves of perfume. I should like this book to be a journey through past and present ages for my readers, a journey that at times resembles a walk in that park and evokes the feeling that they are the guests of a manufacturer of perfumes and spells.

Another of my friends is a pediatrician. He thinks that the toxicosis of babies that so often leads to death is really suicide, a spiritual and corporal self-sacrifice which stems from the little creature's fear of loneliness. In fact, during the first few months of its life, we do leave the baby lying flat, enclosed between boards or bars and gazing at a blank ceiling. No sooner has it got used to its mother's fond look, than we lay it back in the position of a corpse. My friend has applied for the patent of a bed on an inclined plane that puts an end to the baby's isolation and links it constantly with its mother's presence and the objects of everyday life. It is only a modest invention, reminiscent, incidentally of ancient traditions, but it can prevent mental anguish and sometimes even death. In the same way that my doctor friend tried to help children, I should like this book to help the reader to escape from the boards, the bars and the blank ceiling and avoid the poison of isolation.

*Circa* 1920, the Russian poet Valeri Brussov, a contemporary of the October Revolution, seeing one world finish and another begin, wrote: "The origins of cultures that were so different and so widely dispersed as the Aegean, Egyptian, Babylonian, Etruscan, Indian, Aztec and Pacific show similarities that cannot wholly be explained by borrowing and imitation. At the bases of what we look on as the oldest cultures of mankind we must look for a single influence from which all their remarkable analogies sprang. We must look back beyond antiquity for an X, for a still unknown cultural world that set the engine we know in motion. The Egyptians, the Babylonians, the Greeks and Romans were all our teachers. But who were the teachers' teachers?"

During the past fifty years a large number of discoveries have pushed the history of man and his cultures very much further back in time, yet Brussov's question is still valid. Our book does not answer this question definitively, but perhaps it gets a little nearer to the solution of the mystery, to the "teachers' teachers."

We have undertaken this study in the hope that one day there will be a team better equipped to continue it than we are. Until recently the problem dealt with here was the province of fools, charlatans and spiritualists, who based themselves on occult revelations. We want to

13

try to liberate the question of the existence of eternal man from ridicule and at the same time to appease the wrath of archaeologists and anthropologists. That is not so easy, for one does not shake the foundations of academic sciences with impunity, especially as its leaders are convinced that they have established irrefutable theories. One can excavate past cultures, but only so long as one does not bring to light an unconventional idea about the history of mankind in the process.

Scholars seem to agree that our ancestors, clad in leaves and skins, spent thousands of years banging stones together, while waiting for the spark. They also agree that all cultures are mortal. But they do not agree with the idea that human intelligence and skill could have reached the heights several times in the course of millions of years. We shun freedom and the infinite. We need a rather narrow determinism and the certainty that the age of man's mind is comparatively recent in comparison with the age of the earth. The spiritualists among us look on man as an animal who has been given the gift of conceiving of eternity—but not very long ago. The materialists see man as the product of history—but history is young.

But why must humanity and its history necessarily be young? Why this limitation, instead of the idea of perpetual recurrence, the eternity of man? Is there any proof that all cultures are irrevocably mortal? We know far too few of them to establish a law. There are cultures that apparently flowered for thousands of years. Some of the cultures that we call primitive have already existed for so long that they seem to have no beginning and no end. Are they immortal then? Might not the truth be that during past ages man has often tried to climb the rungs of the ladder that lead to a high immortal culture, but has slipped and fallen? Perhaps we are even now in the process of building a culture that will know immortality on earth and in heaven. This optimistic theory will bring a tired smile to many people's lips, for today a cynical doom-ridden attitude is the fashion. But firstly, we all know that fashion soon goes out of date. Secondly, we should be very stupid if we were to stop at such a small rest-house as the moment of the present on such a long and wonderful journey. Thirdly, during the days when we began writing this book, challenging forward-looking slogans like these appeared on the walls of the Sorbonne: "Professors, you are turning us into old people!" and "All power to imagination!" There's something that speaks out loud and clear against the tired smile!

This book lays absolutely no claim to scientific value nor is it intended to be a doctrine of wisdom. Our tool is imagination, and imagination, like science for that matter, sucks nectar wherever it finds it in order to make honey. Science produces miracles or at least tries to do so in all sincerity. Imagination produces miracles or at least tries to do so with the same sincerity. And perhaps there is some truth in the miraculous. If anyone said to me, "There is nothing miraculous to be found in the world" (misusing scientific authority, for as far as I know it is not its job to make men despair), I should obstinately refuse to accept it. With my passionate interest and feeble powers, I should continue to look for the miraculous. And if I did not find anything miraculous in this world, I should say when I left it that my soul was too petty and my intellect too blind, but I should not say that there was nothing miraculous to be found.

Since the publication of *le Matin des magiciens*, undeterred by the imitation or the belittling of our ideas, we have collected and checked new material sent to us by several hundred correspondents all over the world, including scientists and laymen. We should like to thank them all. Our special thanks go to Paul-Emile Victor, leader of the French Polar expedition, who contributed the chapter about the mystery of Piri Reis's maps, and also to our friend Aimé Michel, who allowed us to reprint his article about Leroi-Gourhan's theories of cave

15

art. We are also very grateful to Mme. Freddy Bémont, Lecturer in the Faculty of Literature at the University of Nanterre, for the help she gave us in writing the chapters on Numinor, Catal Hüyük and the Empire of Daedalus.

# PART ONE

## A Pleasure Trip in Eternity

# 1 Doubts about the Theory of Evolution

Two large paintings hang in the lobby of the Athenaeum, the London club frequented by old gentlemen who belong to the Anglo-Saxon intellegentsia. They are portraits of Charles Darwin and his friend and colleague, Thomas Henry Huxley.

One fine afternoon in June, 1963, I sat in the club library having tea with the nephew of one of these two men who had founded a religion. I am not being ironical or exaggerating when I say that they founded a religion. For it is becoming obvious today that the theory of evolution formulated by them more than a hundred years ago could be the starting-point for a new religion.

I said to Julian Huxley, the nephew: "You made a startling remark at the Darwin Centenary Congress held in Chicago in 1958. You said that the evolutionary viewpoint enables us to recognize the main features of a new religion that will meet the needs of ages to come."

"Yes," agreed Sir Julian. "The world is waiting for a new religion and they are pretty sure that there already is something like a ready-made religion, or rather (if I exclude God and a divine finality) an uplifting feeling of a relationship with the universe. Today the individual sciences are so far developed that a conspectus of them provides a new picture of the universe and the potential development of mankind.

"But can the enlargement of our knowledge of man's evolution produce a new religious consciousness?" I asked.

"I know that many people object to the word 'religion',

but even so-called materialistic philosophies such as Marxism have their typically religious aspects."

I thought of Sir Julian's prickly colleague J. B. S. Haldane, who came from an old English family with a tradition of scholarship. At first a convinced Communist, at the end of his career, in India, he studied the physiology of Yogis in ecstasy. He once wrote to me:

"We must reckon with the possibility of a new religion emerging with a creed in harmony with modern thinking, or more accurately with the thinking of a preceding generation. We already find traces of such a profession of faith in the works of the spiritualists, in the economic dogma of the Communist Party and the books of thinkers who believe in creative evolution."

Mentally I saw myself back again in a small study in Rome, belonging to Professor Assaglioli, the master of psychosynthesis: "Today there is one important and significant fact," he said. "It is the expectation of a great religious revival."

These conversations took place before the emergence in the capitals of Europe of young people who were simultaneously revolutionary and antagonistic to progress, who were thirsting for something holy and mystical in the original sense of the word. Perhaps I have something of the clairvoyant in me, perhaps I am merely more receptive to the challenge of the future. At all events, during my conversation with Sir Julian Huxley, I was suddenly convinced that the religious revival would surely come. The only question was what would happen to the evolutionary dogma that had helped to guide two or three generations through the age when God was eclipsed? Apparently Haldane and Huxley had no ready-made answer. Well, we only had to be bold about it, I said to myself, and the dogma might dissolve like the biscuit I was dipping in my tea.

Our grandfathers decreed God's death, but the Trinity withstood the blow. Only the words have changed. The

Father has become evolution, the Son progress and the Holy Ghost history.

Kill the Father once and for all! In other words, cast doubt on evolution. The concept of progress has lost its absolute validity. Consequently history need no longer be unquestioningly considered as a steady upward progression. Once Messianism has been taken away, it is reduced to a chronicle pure and simple. Perhaps this is the real landscape behind the taboos? A harsh landscape? No doubt, but a landscape for free, grown-up men.

Naturally, the adherents of evolution have to be treated with care and respect. They put up a hard fight in the last century. "God created every living creature after its kind," it says in *Genesis*. Less than a hundred years ago an Anglican bishop screamed: "No! There is no evolution. God created the world in six days, *including the fossils!*" And the so-called monkey trial at Dayton, Tennessee, when a teacher was accused because she had taught the theory of evolution, took place as late as 1926. Since then the church has incorporated the most important principles of anthropology into its world-picture. After a neo-Darwinistic analysis of the anatomical development of man during the geological eras, a recently published encyclopedia with Christian leanings says:

"The discovery of human fossils from the Tertiary and Quaternary, the last two geological eras, supply proof that the human body took part in the evolution of the whole living world. In its presentday form it represents the last stage of development in this process. Science can establish the vital moment when the human body, in so far as it differs from an animal body, appeared in its actual form: namely, shortly before the transitional period that led from the Tertiary to the Quaternary, about one million years ago. It was at that moment, after the animal and vegetable world had undergone a long development, that the being of flesh and spirit called man was born by the creative act of god and could begin an individual evolution."

21

Thus the modern Church accepts the theory that man, or at least his body, is a product of evolution. The Church is a little more reserved about his soul. At a certain stage of development, an animal emerged that was extraordinarily like man. Then God suddenly intervened and said, "This is my image; we add the finishing touches and grant this privileged creature 'an independent evolution'."

The history of evolutionary thought is indeed a history of misunderstandings, as the cultural sociologist Emmanuel Berl has shown in his splendid essay *The Evolution of Evolution* (1964).

The celebrated Cuvier was nauseated by the very idea of the theory of evolution, although he himself had contributed a great deal to its future by founding palaeontology, the study of extinct animals. Cuvier believed that any animal could be reconstructed from one small bone. He imagined a natural architecture of the various species, a kind of "golden section" of the diplodocus or the giraffe. Were the multiplication of the species, the disappearance of hundreds of forms of life and the appearance of new forms really foreseen in the plan of a great architect? The supporters of transformism, on the contrary, postulated a close connection of cause and effect, and the emergence of species according to a natural, meaningful need.

Lamarck's doctrine of finalism, like that of Geoffroy Saint-Hilaire, implied a decisive environmental influence. Living creatures changed because environment and living conditions forced them to. Adaptation was the determining factor. It supplied the giant reptiles with paws and warmed their blood when the waters receded. A branch of their descendants became birds. Under the influence of the gradually increasing oxygen content in the air their scales gradually turned into feathers. The representatives of zoology, botany and anthropology (still in its infancy) expressed strong doubts. They could not understand how different species could interbreed. Nevertheless transformism was very plausible. Just as man discovers tools, necessity creates the organ. The snail creates feelers in the same way that the blind man cuts himself a stick; the giraffe grows a long neck so as to be able to reach dates. But the entomologist Jean Henri Fabre justifiably asked himself what bees lived on before they learnt how to make honey. "Lamarck," wrote his opponent Cuvier, "unfortunately belonged to the class of scholars which has in fact made genuine discoveries, but cannot resist blending them with fantastic ideas. The theory of evolution is a large and handsome edifice but alas it rests on an imaginary foundation."

Nevertheless, this theory was to prevail. Undeniably the history of living things had unfolded inconsistently, but there was no proof that the Lamarckian doctrine was the right explanation for all the miracles of evolution. Indeed, it would hardly have prevailed, had not Darwin underpinned it 50 years later with his theory of natural selection, by advocating a mechanistic explanation of the transformation of the species. Imperceptible mutations accumulate and nature makes her choice. But what wonderful stroke of luck enables nature to create such a perfect organ as the eye of the higher vertebrates? Darwin admitted that the very thought of it sent shivers down his spine. In order to amass experience, he made "crazy experiments," such as playing the trumpet to climbing plants. But neither the theory of imperceptible mutation, nor that of sudden mutations (put forward by the Dutchman Hugo de Vries) could give a definitive explanation of the principle of natural selection and ultimately of systematic evolution. Even Henri Bergson and the best scholars of his day admitted that they had no idea of the mechanism by which this evolution worked. Bergson's conclusion was a remarkable *coup de théâtre*. Since we cannot explain the evolution of phenomena, phenomena must be explained by evolution. As we do not know how evolution formed the human eye, all the more reason to say that evolution *did* form it. There is no need for determining mechanisms, since evolution itself does the determining.

Previously genetics had already dealt transformism a fatal blow, without completely shattering belief in the steady upward progress of evolution. August Weismann's theory of chromosomes and the Mendelian laws made hay of the theories of mutation that had come to the aid of transformism. The law of heredity asserts that inherited characteristics are invariable and that acquired characteristics cannot be inherited, because heredity is not transmitted from organism to organism but from sperm-cell to sperm-cell. Consequently, genetics is no help to the theory of evolution.

The "transformists" at the beginning of the nineteenth century thought that it was quite enough to have replaced the arbitrary will of the creator by a rational hypothesis. They never had anything to say about the possible meaning of evolution. Causes produced effects, the influence of environment and natural selection made the species transform themselves, the forms of life developed from the amoeba down to man in obedience to inexorable needs. To transformists it would have been unscientific to ask if evolution had a meaning. Their doctrine was neither pessimistic nor optimistic. They refused to endow a natural phenomenon with a purpose and a goal. Somewhat obtusely they held the balance between hope and despair, and they had a certain tendency to make painful admissions. The natural sciences presented a somewhat cheerless aspect during this period. Nietzsche drew gloomy inspiration for his tragic philosophy of life from the determinism which decides the evolution of the species. He became dismally enraptured with the pitiless force of natural selection and saw mankind on top of a gigantic cemetery of extinct species.

The biologists, who "had not seen God in their testtubes," would shrug their shoulders under their black frock-coats if anyone tried to attribute a meaning to natural phenomena. And the psychologists themselves sided with them. God and the virtues were products like alcohol and sugar. Genesis said that we came from dust and promised us that we should return to dust. Religious dogma claimed that we were dust animated by God. But to the natural scientists we were not created by the will of the Lord, we were simply primates developed by the play of blind chance, pitched aimlessly into a nature that has no goal and is condemned to extinction, anyway, by the first law of thermo-dynamics.

If, for some reason, the discoveries of modern genetics had been made before the industrial revolution, there would never have been any talk of the *élan vital*, the vital impulse, as the organically developing force in Bergson's philosophy, not to mention "creative evolution." Principles of the sublime immutability of nature would have won the day and our whole outlook on living things, the history of mankind and its cultures, and of our own civilization would have altered accordingly.

But in the meantime the idea of evolution had combined with the idea of progress. With the emergence of the industrial society and its first impressive achievements, the idea that paradise lies behind us disappeared. Steam engines and electricity transferred it from the past to the future. Man would "win the victory over nature"; things would change and so would man. Progress would be irresistible. Mankind could hope and find a meaning in history. Hegel established the metaphysics of progress and Marx his own anthropology.

The central doctrine of Lamarckism that the environment determines change and that the function creates the organ is found again in "scientific socialism." And if it is Marx who explains that men make their discoveries at the moment when they need them, it is Lamarck who is putting the words into his mouth. The inexorable laws of "economic development" are still transformism and the principle of class struggle is the cousin of natural selection.

The idea of creative evolution is an intellectual invention intended to give an account of a general history of living things whose mechanism cannot be explained. And this idea is intended to justify all the sacrifices the blossoming industrial society demands in the name of progress. Progress is the radiant heritage of the whole of evolution, the sparkling end-product of 3,000,000,000 years of life. It illuminates the world. Before it the world was dark, or, to be more precise, man did not know the light of day. Hence the expression "the century of Enlightenment." It is the century in which the idea of progress made its appearance. At last our age has come, at last we appear and take further development upon ourselves, we, who, during a slow process when matter matured, were linked by the fear and terror, and chemical influences we shared, with the prehistoric animals that vegetated in the swampy waters of the Devonian.

We no longer doubt that progress is justified by evolution, but we must not forget that this certainty was implanted by the imperatives of our industrial and technical civilization rather than by a scientifically illuminated reality.

Emmanuel Berl is quite right when he speaks in this connection of the pressure "which is put on the champion of creative evolution by the civilization surrounding him." It is this, he continues, "that undoubtedly confers on the idea of evolution and progress a value which bears no relation to the phenomena actually established. It is this which sends researchers in the right direction, by paralyzing our mistrust of words that mean and suggest far more than they express; it is this which leads to blending a theory that is acceptable like all theories, but also controversial, with a complex of well-established facts. These facts can clarify priority in time, succession and causalities, but they certainly cannot show any final goal and still less the ultimate meaning of the processes that have not yet finished and whose outcome no one can foresee.

"We do not know the outcome of the struggle which life is carrying on against itself and inanimate matter;

we are incapable of knowing it. The biologists did not foresee the atom bomb, nor do they know what new viruses might decimate the human race tomorrow. So their evolutionism includes an act of faith—an act of faith that does not even quote a revelation as its authority, and which becomes all the more difficult to accept the more the transmission of acquired characteristics is excluded. In professing evolution, biologists imagine that they are directing and dominating sociology, whereas really they are obeying it. For it is sociology and not biology from which evolution gets its attraction and the prestige it enjoys. It is the progress of man, not that of animal and vegetable species, which we take for granted in our work and in our thinking.

"And if we are inclined to believe that everything in the world will get better and better, it is because we see the power man wields in the world getting bigger and bigger. But whatever standpoint we adopt, it would surely be to everybody's advantage if we approached evolution more suspiciously and used the word more cautiously, after thinking about it first. How can we predict what purpose evolution will serve tomorrow? Evolution that has become pious, if not downright orthodox, after having been such a daring freethinker? We are no longer sure that it brings its followers happiness. Poets taught us long ago that man can inflict torture by hope, and both historians and heads of state can certainly make modern life more excruciating in the name of the better future they promise. The worst tyrannies become excusable, even justifiable, if it is taken for granted that by a happy dispensation the world is moving towards a paradisal state. When everything that happens is tending towards the good, there is no more evil. A gigantic blood-bath will not hold up the course of evolution; some people may even flatter themselves that it will speed it up and that a trivial massacre of nine hundred million men will bring the survivors close to the classless society which socialism aims at. In the same way, the Nazis claimed that by eliminating the inferior races they would accelerate and perfect the beneficial play of natural selection. Evolutionism is no less subject to madness than any other 'ism'. We must watch over it very carefully, especially if we intend to support it."

And what if evolution were a Russian doll, concealing several fully formed evolutions from us, one inside the other? If, for example man had made his appearance several times? And if man's various attempts to dominate nature had had several beginnings? What if we were on the right track this time? Naturally this idea has its share of extravagance, but the incessant backdating of the beginning of human history in recent years provides rich food for such fantasies. Modern biologists, writes Gaston Bouthoul in his book *Social Variations and Mutations*, published in 1969, incline to the view that nature did not create any new animal species during the last geological eras. Lucien Couénot (*L'Evolution biologique*, 1951) estimates that nature's creative impulse seems to have stopped five hundred million years ago, with the appearance of birds. No new form of life has been added since the primates and man. Yet the average density of radiation does not seem to have altered. Apparently nothing in our physical environment has changed essentially. So what are we to make of evolution as a continuing process? "The observations of modern biology," continues Bouthoul, "make the emergence of mutations from which new species arise seem doubtful."

The American zoologist Thomas H. Morgan has subjected insects to the most varied kinds of treatment, including bombardment with rays which reproduced the physical conditions in the oldest geological periods, without achieving convincing signs of a mutation.

However, the human race did change its ability to act and its way of life in the space of a few centuries. Here again we link up with evolution, which to us is inseparably bound up with the idea of progress, by declaring that "the creation of machines and techniques are genuine biological mutations of the human race," and that even if ascending evolution has not influenced *homo* in general, it has at least had an effect on *homo sapiens* and his societies. Just as if nature suddenly tiring, as if the engine of progressive evolution had suffered a breakdown, had delegated its functions to *homo sapiens*. And as we are evolutionists in spite of everything, we fall back on the article of faith of a father of church, St. Clement of Alexandria: "Once the creation was finished, the destiny of nature was entrusted to men."

So perhaps if we tracked down the traces of an evolution, we should actually find some. But exclusively in man. And in that case we should have to accept the idea that man is an exceptional creation, belonging to a privileged species. "Today many biologists are of the opinion that the spontaneous mutations that have now disappeared in animal species, continue in the human brain, mainly in the cortical zone, so that changes in mentality would be nothing else but the psychosociological aspect of these spontaneous mutations of mysterious, and perhaps cosmic origin." (Bouthoul.)

From this point of view, we should also have to assert in opposition to the general theory of evolution, that man is an exceptional animal who constitutes a form of life outside the overall process. We feel strongly tempted to make such an assertion, at our own risk. At the same time we should add that this form of life, which is outside the general process, might easily have emerged, not in the course of a slow evolution, but more rapidly, and *every time conditions were suitable.*

*In the history of our planet man may have appeared many times in the course of the past millions of years, so that we could say that man is eternal, measured by the duration of our civilizations.* This hypothesis is not mystical. It does not postulate an arbitrary, watchful God who creates man anew whenever conditions permit. If anything, it is a natural hypothesis. Just as chance plays no part in chemistry, it would be unlikely to do so in evolution. Just as permanent molecules exist, there would be at least one permanent form of life, man, who would appear constantly, whenever the opportunity allowed, and who would experience many vicissitudes, many transformations and many heights and depths in the eternal striving for a higher form of being.

Every time that new finds are made, the birthday of the first man is pushed further and further back. In September 1969, an Anthropological and Palaeontological Congress held in the UNESCO building in Paris rejected the idea that Neanderthal man was our ancestor and advanced the theory that a man who made tools and worshipped the dead had existed more than 2,000,000 years ago. But today that is still inadequate. Excavations in the Chad (northern Central Africa) have revealed men who were 6,000,000 years old. We could go on searching endlessly and finally come to the conclusion that by our criteria there is no more a first man than there is a limit to the universe.

We are not claiming that the birth of man coincided with the appearance of life on earth more than 3,000,-000,000 years ago. But perhaps the human race could have appeared 10,000,000 years ago, then disappeared owing to natural catastrophes, only to reappear later, just as life gradually returns to islands that have become barren because of volcanic eruptions.

"Darwin's explanation of the transformation of the species by slow, step by step mutations is difficult to accept. A characteristic that has not had time to assert itself, that only exists in its embryonic state, is generally inviable, and indeed more of an impediment in the struggle for existence. Thus it is condemned to disappear. So how can this totality which is a completely new being have developed step by step?" That is what the natural philosopher Heinrich Schirmbeck asks himself in his book *You Will be like Gods. Man in the Biological Revolution*

(1966). However, he does not doubt, basing himself on anthropological data, that man "as an element of nature, has a biological past whose roots are deep in primordial animal forms."

However, scholars who have come up against the impossibility of explaining man's genesis evolutively have not been slow to get around the obstacle by isolating man from the rest of the universe and attributing a personal development to him from the beginning. Thus the Munich prehistorian, Edgar Dacqué, claims that man should not be considered as the final form of a long development, but as the "first-born" and centre of creation. According to Dacqué, man is the first created being and the whole of creation proliferated around this original model.

Compared with this hypothesis, our own is less fantastic. It assumes a constant form of life which appears and disappears, depending on whether the circumstances are right or not. In other words, one that returns on several occasions with the passage of time. Is our theory really as extravagant as Dacqué's? Now that the span of "human" ages is growing steadily longer as the result of anthropological research, we are at least entitled to seek for other explanations besides evolutionism.

In 1856, when the first fragments of the skeleton of Neanderthal man were discovered, there were scholars who said that man's family tree did not go anything like so far back and that they were the remains of a wild beast. During the last century remains of fossil men and ape men from quite different periods have been excavated all over the world and yet it is not always easy to distinguish between them and establish a family tree. Today we look on the Neanderthal man who made the delicate tools of the Mousterian, a phase of the Upper Palaeolithic, as an episode in human history 50,000 years ago. He may have been a product of interbreeding between an infinitely older *homo habilis,* or an already existing *homo*

31

*sapiens,* and *pithecanthropi,* in other words a mixture like Solo man in Java.

In 1948, Dr. Leakey, who has been excavating in East Africa for forty years, found in Kenya the traces of one of the first links in the chain which is supposed to have produced the primates and man—traces which are supposed to be about forty to twenty-five million years old. In 1959, Dr. Leakey discovered the oldest then known hominid, *Zinjanthropus australopithecus,* who lived in the region of Olduvai (in present-day Tanzania) 180,000 to 800,000 years ago. In 1962, he discovered *Kenyapithecus* who goes back about 50,000,000 years and probably also belongs to the ancestors of the hominids. In 1963 he claimed that the new discovery of *homo habilis* at Olduvai called all the theories of man's origin in question.

"The discovery of a creature with characteristics so closely resembling human ones, although it lived nearly two million years ago, is in itself a revolution," wrote Yvonne Rebeyrol in *Le Monde,* on the occasion of the UNESCO congress. Until now the race of hominids progressed from the uncouth *australopithecus* to *homo sapiens* (i.e. present-day man), who first appeared about 25,000 years ago. Previously the most important links in evolution were *pithecanthropus,* who was later and more highly developed than *australopithecus,* and Neanderthal man, who was more primitive than *homo sapiens.* And now a new creature has come to light that is as old as *australopithecus,* but exhibits striking similarities to *homo sapiens.* In Dr. Leakey's view, *homo habilis* is our only ancestor, the other hominids being merely unsuccessful products that had no descendants. *Australopithecus, pithecanthropus* and *homo habilis* appeared simultaneously, but only *homo habilis* was the starting-point of the fruitful development that led to *homo sapiens.* Moreover, says Leakey, in various places, mainly Great Britain, France, Germany and Hungary, there have been finds of fossil skulls whose characteristics are reminiscent of modern man, but which come from very ancient levels. Only very recently, two quite "modern" skulls were excavated from the bed of the river Omo (Ethiopia) that were also very old. This dispersion of already highly developed forms apparently indicates the widespread diffusion of *homo habilis*.

"However, Dr. Leakey thinks that man was born in the region comprising East Africa, Arabia and the west of India. In India archaeologists have already found a fossil ape, *ramapithecus*, which is younger but not far removed from *Kenyapithecus*, and signs of primitive industries have also been discovered. So Leakey is convinced that systematic excavations in India or Arabia would be extremely successful, since East Africa has already shown how rich it is in fossils. The longitude and latitude of this part of the world were exceptionally favorable for the emergence and development of primitive hominids. Its volcanic soil is ideal for the preservation of fossils. The more scholars seek, the more they find. Quite recently, Mrs. Leakey has dug up at Olduvai a skull of *homo habilis* which is apparently quite or almost complete. And Dr. Leakey has produced a tooth which he found on Kenyan territory, south of Lake Rudolf. This tooth probably belonged to a hominid who lived 8,000,000 years ago."

However, Leakey assumes that *homo sapiens* could not have appeared minus the ability to kindle fire, i.e. "having the security, the inner repose, which could produce abstract ideas. Tools are demonstrable very early, but they are not decisive for the transition from preman to man. To put it more precisely, man entered life with abstract thought, and the concepts of magic, religion and art." In Leakey's opinion, the transition from *homo habilis* to *homo sapiens*, who is not more than 100,000 years old, must have taken a considerable time.

This theory does not rest on definitive knowledge. It merely replaces uncertainties by vague estimations. The only certainty is that the more we seek, the more we find. For example, a *homo sapiens* who is 100,000 years old, a *homo habilis* who is several millions of years old. Datings

33

change every six months and the most recent conclusions of research are called in question again. We are swimming in a sea of time. But if hominids lived more than 8,000,000 years ago, the classical theory of evolution has gone bankrupt. And if there were thinking men 100,000 years ago, then from a rational point of view we must ask ourselves whether we can swallow the proposition that there is only a single enlightened moment in this long adventure, namely the last five-hundredth part of man's stay on earth.

Perhaps it would be a useful mental exercise to leave out of account for once this proposition that only the last five-hundredth part of previous humanity has made us masters of the whole of thinking humanity of earlier times, and adopt the opposite position—that of seeing ourselves less as an exception in the history of mankind and more as an exception in the history of living things. Let us accept the idea that man might be an immutable form who appeared repeatedly, with his apogees and his catastrophes. In this concept and in the feeling that mankind might be a permanent species on the earth and in the universe lies a chance to influence future culture, society and morals.

# 2 The Continental Drift

Traces of organic matter were discovered in the rock samples that the astronauts brought back from the moon. Did they come from the moon? Or had they been introduced by the astronauts, in spite of all the precautionary measures. We still know very little about the nature of the matter of our satellite. But do we know everything about the earth on which we live? By no means. Its depths are virtually unknown. Its history is still a puzzle.

Look at a map of the world. Doesn't it look like a jigsaw puzzle, the parts of which have been dislodged? The east coast of the Americas seems to have come loose from the west of Europe and Africa. Were the two land masses gradually driven apart until a sea appeared—the 3,000-mile-wide Atlantic Ocean? And what about the Indian Ocean? Are South Africa, Madagascar, the Antarctic and Australia parts of the jigsaw puzzle, too? Geologists have long been struck by the similarity of the rock formations found in South Africa, in the Deccan, Madagascar and Brazil. Some scholars have put forward the theory of an original continent called Gondwana.[1] According to this hypothesis, the whole southern hemisphere was covered in the Precambrian by a single mainland block, which broke up into the separate continents of this hemisphere in the Mesozooic. In 1969, the skull of a lystrosaurus was found in the Antarctic, in the Alexandra mountains. This is a reptile that lived at the beginning of the Mesozooic. Similar fossils have been found in South Africa and Australia. Lastly, there are unmistakable similarities between the fossil flora of the Antarctic, South Africa, Australia and South America.

[1] Named after the Gonds, a Dravidian people of Central Asia.

And the coal in the Antarctic contains fossils of large trees that once flourished in tropical climates.

In 1914, the German geophysicist and meteorologist, Alfred Wegener, put forward a hypothesis about the earth's surface. According to his theory, all the continents originally formed a single land mass. Then several divisions took place and the separate continents were driven apart. Wegener died in 1930 on an expedition to Greenland. His theory was discarded.

In 1969, Patrick M. Hurley, a Professor of Geology, declared: "I have carried on my research in order to prove that Wegener's theory is absurd." But he had to admit that the German scholar was right about one essential fact. The continents *do* shift.

In fact, since 1950 new conclusions have been reached that lend more and more weight to the theory of the mobility of the earth's crust and the continental shift. The following is an account of these conclusions.

Palaeomagnetism is the geophysical term for the study of the direction and intensity of magnetism in rocks. The importance of this magnetization consists in the fact that it is oriented in the direction of the earth's magnetic field at the time when the rock cooled. Thus the proof of the orientation of the earth's magnetic field at any given time is contained in the sedimentary rock. During studies of ancient European rock formations, it was discovered that the older the rock, the further the positions of the palaeomagnetic pole were from the position of the present-day geographic pole. Four hundred million year old rock reveals a pole at the Equator. Accordingly, either the magnetic poles or the continents have shifted.

The examination of rock from the same period in different continents ought to have given the same position for the pole. But the result of the experiments was different. Instead of coinciding, the palaeomagnetic poles of North America regularly lay west of the European ones. The only explanation for this would be that North America had moved westward in relation to Europe. Which brings us back to the theory of continental shift.

In the same way, the previous poles of the southern continents do not agree with the poles of the northern hemisphere. But with one difference. Other factors indicated that the countries of the southern hemisphere had moved further away from each other than the northern ones.

The magnetic directions obtained from glacier-deposited sedimentary rock in Central Africa shift the south pole to the Republic of South Africa. Similar data in Australia move the south pole for the same period to the southern part of Australia. If these data about the position of the south pole three hundred million years ago are correct, Australia in those days must have been situated somewhat further north and nearer to the east coast of South Africa. That would strengthen the theory according to which all countries formed a single mass 3,000,000 years ago.

Wegener's theory was taken up again by the American Professor, Charles W. Hapgood, and supported by no less a scientist than Albert Einstein, who wrote in the post-humously published introduction to Hapgood's book *Earth Shifting Crust* (1958): "I often get letters from people who want to consult me about their still unpublished ideas. Naturally, these ideas seldom have any scientific value. But I am very enthusiastic about Hapgood's theory. His idea is original and extremely illuminating, and if his assertions are strengthened by proof, they will be of the utmost importance for everything connected with the history of the earth's surface.

"Numerous experimental data indicate that abrupt changes of climate occur at those points on the earth's surface where studies have been carried out with reliable means. Hapgood gives an explanation for this. The earth's rigid crust is subjected from time to time to considerable shifts over the viscous, plastic and possibly fluid inner layer. Such shifts can take place under the influence of comparatively weak forces on the crust. These forces again may originate from the rotation of the earth, the axis of which has a tendency to shift.

"In one polar zone the ice is deposited constantly, but it is not distributed symmetrically around the poles. The rotation of the earth affects these ice masses irregularly and produces a centrifugal force which is transmitted to the earth's rigid crust. When it has reached a certain intensity, this centrifugal force makes the earth's crust slide over the rest of the terrestrial body, as a result of which the polar regions are pushed nearer the Equator.

"There is no doubt that the earth's crust is resistant enough not to collapse under the weight of the ice sheet. The question remains whether the earth's crust can actually slide over the inner layers.

"The author has not confined himself to a brief exposition of this idea. He has also offered ample material to confirm his theory. In my opinion, this astonishing, genuinely exciting thesis merits the serious attention of everyone who is concerned with the problem of the earth's development."

Hapgood assumes that there is a viscous, fluid layer under the earth's crust on which the continents move like skates. In fact, seismography indicates that the interior of the earth is composed as follows:

an outer crust, some 21 miles deep, narrowing to 7 miles under the sea;

The "mantle," a region which extends from the base of the crust to a depth of 1,800 miles and comprises a rigid zone of about 60 miles (the lithosphere), a partially molten zone of some hundred miles (the asthenosphere) and a wholly rigid zone (the mesosphere);

The center, whose temperature may be around 6,000°C, whereas the temperature of the border between core and mantle is probably about 4,000°C. The temperature of the lithosphere is constant, but it is higher along a narrow strip on the ocean bed which is called the Mid-Oceanic Ridge.

A further feature of the ocean bed is a series of trenches that surround terra firma to a width of 10 miles and are between 6,600 and 8,750 yards deep. They are the center of pronounced seismical activity.

This model of the interior of the earth is based purely on speculation. It is impossible for us to see the earth in cross-section and so far we have been unable to make deep enough drillings to check our assumptions. So our knowledge is very incomplete and mainly hypothetical. If the earth could be X-rayed one day, we should know if Hapgood was right.

But even if this theory should prove false, the thesis of continental drift has gained in importance from the explanation put forward in 1963 by the two American professors, Hess and Dietz. They assumed that breaks in the earth's mantle take place under the Mid-Oceanic Ridge.

Then a new crust forms on top of this ridge, while the old crust is swallowed up by the ocean trenches. In this way the ocean bed that lies between the ridges and the floor of the trenches would gradually shift.

The idea of an expanding ocean floor is comparatively new. More accurate data in this field would be a valid argument in the long chain of evidence for the shifting of the earth's crust.

If a new crust forms on its surface, then the former crust must be destroyed at some point, so that the earth always maintains the same surface area. According to the theory of the expansion of the ocean floor, this crust is destroyed in the ocean trenches. Earthquakes are especially violent and frequent in the trench system. Moreover, the trenches are the site of the deepest earthquakes, some as deep as 430 miles. The earthquakes connected with the trench system extend over a surface forming an angle

39

of 30° with that of the ocean basin. Many earthquakes take place under the trenches.

Today there is no lack of evidence of the expansion of the ocean floor and the drifting of the earth's crust. In addition, we can observe what happens on the earth's surface on the basis of seismological studies.

*Since the continents drift simultaneously with the ocean floor, it seems unavoidable that two or more continents must collide some day.*

The Mid-Oceanic Ridge is in contact with a land-mass in two places, the Gulf of California and the Red Sea. In both cases this results in strong internal movements. The Red Sea was formed by the separation of the Arabian peninsula from the African continent. Apparently the California peninsula is separating from the mainland at an annual rate of two inches. If it maintains this movement, California will become an island in a few million years.

Today we do not possess enough knowledge of the movements of the earth's mantle. We must await the results of current research. Whatever they may be, the forces which are at work here are of vital concern to the human race. They open up prospects of new fantastic hypotheses about the past and the future.

The explanation put forward by Hess and Dietz (expansion of the ocean floor) seems preferable to Hapgood's thesis of the existence of a fluid viscous layer on which the earth's crust floats. The temperature of the border layer between center and mantle is 4,000°C. One cannot imagine how this temperature could cause a fluid layer on which the continents glide. However, there are many gaps in our knowledge of the qualities of matter which is exposed to high temperatures and great pressure. Hapgood concludes from the finds of tropical fossils in the Antarctic that there was a period when this continent was on the Equator and then driven away from it. Between 10,000 and 15,000 years ago the Antarctic was about 2,500 miles further north. The climate was mild. About this time, an ice-age began, for reasons unknown to us. The ice first accumulated at the pole, then melted and reached the temperate zones. Owing to the centrifugal force produced by the two centers of gravity of the polar caps, the earth's crust began to slide. Hudson Bay and the province of Quebec were displaced 2,500 miles southwards, Siberia northwards and the Antarctic southwards. In a few thousands of years the Antarctic reached the South Pole.

This dating of 10,000 to 15,000 years is not accepted by the majority of geologists. According to geological chronology, the melting of the ice probably took place suddenly, at the most in a couple of thousand years.

However this may be, modern geology makes Wegener's theory seem reasonable. According to it, the continental drift is a reality, even if its working is not yet known. That is to say, whether it is a question of the land-masses sliding on a viscous fluid layer or the expansion of the ocean bed. And if we admit the possibility that great cultures existed in the past and vanished without trace, these geological phenomena should stimulate our imagination more than submerged continents like Atlantis.

Speaking of Atlantis, we favor a theory which says that it was not a continent, but a Cretan colony in the Mediterranean that was destroyed by an eruption of the volcano Santorin about 3000 B.C.

But let us go back to Hapgood. Let us accept his assumption that there was a culture in the Antarctic or that other cultures knew of this continent before the glaciation which caused its comparatively sudden displacement. Perhaps remnants of its slumber under the ice. And the question remains whether other traces of cultures are not buried under the ice in the far north for the same reasons—cultures tallying with the legends of Thule, Numinor and the Hyperboreans.

How did men live on the continent that collapsed? Its

41

geographical extent changed with the passage of the centuries. Earthquakes took place continuously, the climate altered, the fluctuations in temperature must have been unbearable. Ought we not reinterpret the Nordic sagas from this point of view?

"There is something irresistibly romantic in the idea of the vanished cultures, the lost cities, the forgotten discoveries," writes Hapgood. "It is as if man's mind was transported down the corridors of time. It seems as if spacious prospects must suddenly unfold somewhere, at a turn in the corridor—prospects of wonderful cities that perished in their heyday and were erased from the memory of mankind. With a vague presentiment of the eternal recurrence of all things, we seem to hear the words of the magician Prospero in Shakespeare's *Tempest*:

> "And like the baseless fabric of this vision
> The cloud-capped towers, the gorgeous palaces,
> The solemn temples, the great globe itself,
> Yea, all which it inherits, shall dissolve,
> And like this insubstantial pageant faded
> Leave not a wrack behind . . ."

Hapgood thinks that an astonishing discovery should confirm his theory about the Antarctic. I refer to the famous story of the Piri Reis maps.

This remarkable story, first made public in France by Paul-Emile Victor, the leader of the French polar expedition, has already been dealt with in our book *Le Matin des magiciens*. Hapgood's *Maps of the Ancient Sea-Kings*, as well as the conference organized by the University of Georgetown, Washington, with the theme "New and Old Discoveries in Antarctica," and other works, have not actually solved the enigma of these maps, but they have at least enquired into their origin. In July, 1966, we asked Paul-Emile Victor to express his views of the mystery of Piri Reis in our review *Planète*. As his article has not been superceded by more recent research, we should like to insert it in our text at this point.

"I have no hesitation," wrote Paul Emile Victor, "about putting forward daring hypotheses in this article. But I should like to say emphatically that that is all they are. The true scientists are poets and dreamers. Without them there would be no science. The others are book-keepers and tradesmen; they don't discover anything. And anyway, how boring life would be without imagination!"

# 3 The Story of the "Impossible Maps"

Piri Reis's maps have an accurately dated and demonstrable historical background, starting in 1513, and a "prehistoric" background which is not supported by documents. It refers to the period before 1513.

Let us begin with the known facts. On November 9, 1929, Malil Edhem, Director of the Turkish National Museums, discovered in the Topkapi Museum at Istanbul two maps of the world, or more accurately fragments of maps, which everyone believed had been lost. They were the maps of Piri Reis, the celebrated sixteenth-century hero and pirate, who describes their origin in detail in his autobiography *Bahriye*.

His memoirs alone would not have excited any attention, but after the discovery of the maps they became of increasing interest to scholars. However, it was not until the end of the Second World War that a comparative study of the maps and Piri Reis's text was made. Piri Reis, the bold seafarer, made his contribution to strengthening the Ottoman Empire's undisputed mastery of the seas, but he was also an educated and intelligent man. While he hastened from one adventure to another, he found time to write his book *Bahriye*, which is full of vivid descriptions of all the ports in the Mediterranean and is illustrated with 21 maps. He also drew two maps of the world, one in the year 1513 and the other in 1528, in the reign of Suleiman the Great.

Piri Reis was an extremely conscientious cartographer —and he knew it. For he writes in the introduction to *Bahriye* that the preparation of a map requires a thorough grounding in the subject, as well as a special gift. He describes in detail the work on his first map, which he drew in his native town of Gelibolu (Gallipoli) in 1513. He explains that he studied all the maps known to him, some of them very secret and very ancient. There were about twenty in all, and they included oriental maps which he was undoubtedly the only man in Europe to possess at the time.

Because of his knowledge of Greek, Italian, Portuguese and Spanish, he was able to extract the full benefit from the data on the maps. Naturally he also had a map made by Columbus himself, for which he was indebted to one of the famous Genoese explorer's seamen. This sailor had been taken prisoner by Kemal Reis, an uncle of Piri Reis, and thus was able to supplement the Turkish cartographer's knowledge.

Until recently, the book *Bahriye,* as already mentioned, had a purely anecdotal value. To the Turks it was interesting as proof of their great past, to the Europeans as throwing light on the "barbarian pirates." However, even before the maps mentioned in it were known, detailed study of this book had enabled historians to avoid one great mistake: the claim that Columbus discovered America. He rediscovered it, or more accurately, he revealed this continent, the existence of which was hitherto only known to a few initiates, to Europe. The Turkish admiral's evidence is clear and unequivocal. In the chapter about the "Western Sea" (for long the name of the Atlantic Ocean), he talks in detail about the Genoese seafarer, whose adventure he describes as follows:

"An unbeliever called Columbus, who came from Genoa, discovered these lands. A book had come into the hands of this man and he found that it was written in it that at the end of the Western Sea, in the far west, there were coasts and islands and all kinds of metals and also precious stones. After the man had studied the book for a long time, he went to all the notables of Genoa in turn and asked them: 'Give me two ships to voyage and

45

discover these lands.' They said: 'Presumptuous man, how can anyone find a limit to the "Western Sea." It vanishes into the mist and darkness.'

"They said Columbus saw that he could expect nothing from the Genoans and hastened to the Bey of Spain to tell him his story. There he was given the same answer, but he kept on importuning the Spaniards so long that the Bey finally gave him two well-equipped ships and said: 'O Columbus, if what thou sayest comes true, I will make thee Kapudan of this land.' And after he had said this, the king sent Columbus forth on the Western Sea."

Piri Reis then tells the story that a member of Columbus's crew told him. We shall only quote a passage that is relevant to our subject: "The inhabitants of the island saw that nothing evil threatened them from our ships; so they caught fish and brought them to us in their canoes. The Spaniards were very pleased and gave them glass beads, for Columbus had read in his book that these people liked glass beads." This quite astonishing detail, which to the best of our knowledge has not been commented on before, stands out even more if we link it up with the data that are recorded on one of the maps as a key to the symbols used. There Piri Reis asserts that the book which Columbus read belonged to the age of Alexander the Great. It is difficult to assert that the Turkish admiral actually possessed this celebrated book, but at all events he knew about it.

Consequently, Columbus set forth with the intention of discovering America. He believed in his precious book and the future was to confirm that he was right. He gave this confidential information only to the Genoese notables and the king of Spain. Publicly he supported the opinion prevalent at the time that, since the earth was round, anyone who travelled westwards would inevitably return to his point of departure one day, and in the meantime come across the known countries of eastern Europe, but in the reverse order. This view was confirmed by cartographers. There was a map attributed to a certain

Toscanelli which Columbus took on his expedition. It showed the European coasts from right to left, then the "Western Sea" and lastly the island of "Cepanda" (another form of "Cipangu," as Japan was called at the time), the country of "Cathay" (China), India and the south-east Asian islands. America was not drawn on this map. That is why the new world was called the "West Indies".

As it is not our intention to dethrone Columbus, we shall not go into detail about his predecessors, who may equally well have discovered America without realizing the importance of their discovery. The Vikings are the best known of them. But Piri Reis names yet others: Savobrandan,[1] the Portuguese Nicola Giuvan and Antonio the Genoese.

Even before his maps were rediscovered, more attention should have been paid to Piri Reis's notes. He repeatedly states: "There is nothing in this book that is not based on facts." And he is aware "that the slightest error makes a chart unusable." There is no doubt that here speaks a professional, who knows all the ins and outs of navigation. We must bear that in mind when we deal with his maps of the world.

Only parts of these maps have come down to us. They show the Atlantic and its American, African, Arctic and Antarctic coasts. The maps are on colored parchment, illuminated and decorated with many illustrations: portraits of the rulers of Portugal, Morocco and Guinea, an elephant and an ostrich in Africa, lamas and pumas in South America, ships in the ocean and along the coasts, and birds on the islands. The mountains are drawn in relief, the rivers are marked with thick lines, rocky places in black, sandy and shallow waters with red dots and reefs with a cross.

[1] He means the Irish monk Brandan, who is supposed to have sought the "Islands of the Blessed" in the sixth century on a voyage lasting several years.

These, then, were the venerable parchments that were rediscovered in 1929. The Turks looked on them as a national treasure, because they reminded them of the glorious days of the Ottoman Empire, but they did not bother to examine them very closely. Reproductions were acquired by various libraries. In 1953 a Turkish naval officer sent a copy to the head engineer of the Hydrographical Institute of the US Navy, who in turn consulted Arlington H. Mallery, an expert on ancient maps. And that is when the affair of the Piri Reis maps really began. Who is Arlington H. Mallery? As an engineer, he had always been interested in the sea and had served in troop transport in World War Two. When he had finished his military service, he devoted his leisure time to a subject which was close to his heart—the pre-Columbian discovery of America. After linguistic research (to prove the borrowings the Iroquois tongue had made from the Old Norwegian), an intensive study of the Scandinavian sagas, archaeological investigations and consultation of old maritime atlases, the so-called *portulans,* he was able to retrace the adventures of the Vikings, described in their epics, in Iceland, Greenland, Newfoundland and the coastal region of Canada. He described his discoveries in a book published in 1951, *The Lost America,* which met with a favorable reception. Mallery defended the thesis that there had been an iron culture in America not only before the European conquest, but possibly even before the Indian population.

But this was only the beginning of an exciting adventure. When Piri Reis's maps reached him, Mallery was already quite an expert in the field. He saw at first glance that this find put all the others in the shade and realized intuitively that the maps concealed a fascinating secret.

The first problem was to decipher the maps, that is to say, to find out the system of projection used. After years of work, a Swedish scholar, Nordenskjöld, had translated the old charts into modern cartographical language. His work served first Mallery and then Charles Hapgood and his pupils as a foundation. They recognized the different provenances of the prototypes of Piri Reis's maps and were able to reconstruct a great deal of the originals. This labor, checked by mathematicians, should be the best proof that the Piri Reis maps constituted a real problem. A great deal of evidence to prove the maps' antiquity has been produced. Here is an example: The lama drawn on the maps was not known to Europeans in the first decade of the sixteenth century. Not even Columbus could calculate degrees of longitude, which are accurately drawn on the maps. Comparison with other contemporary maps shows how unusual they are. The difference strikes one at once. We quote a few such maps. Jean Severo's map, published at Leyden in 1514, is correct for Europe and Africa, but it is noticeable that Central and North America are one uniform land-mass. The map ascribed to Lopa Hamen and published in 1519 is no better. The dimensions of America are out of scale in relation to Africa and the outlines of the New World are scarcely recognizable.

Another map, drawn by an unknown Portuguese, appeared in 1520. South America comes to a stop in southern Brazil. We must bear in mind that Magellan did not circumnavigate America until that year, so that the results of his voyage of discovery could not have been known.

A map of America that was published in 1544, almost forty years after Piri Reis, in Sebastian Munster's *Kosmographie*, is still unsatisfactory, although the new world is identified as a continent on it.

So we see that the claims in *Bahriye* were strengthened by the maps. Piri Reis possessed undeniably valuable information about America that was older than Columbus's. How much older? That is the great question.

Now we must look at the modern interpretations of these maps. We are faced with two theories, the American and the Russian. First of all let us follow Mallery, who discovered the secret, and Hapgood, who tried to solve it.

The deciphering of the astonishingly accurately drawn

49

part of the map which comprised the sections between north and south Brazil presented no difficulty. As regards the north and south of the map, Mallery was convinced, once that the old indications had been "translated" into the language of modern cartography, that on the one hand Piri Reis had drawn the coastline of the Antarctic and on the other that Greenland and the Antarctic had been drawn as they had been before the glaciation of the poles.

A bold hypothesis like this can only be advanced if one is in a position to define the shape of the solid land base of the Arctic and Antarctic which exists under the ice.

New knowledge in this field has been acquired quite recently. Modern techniques (gravimetry, seismographical measurements) that were developed by the French polar expedition and used both in Greenland and the Antarctic produced startling results.

Firstly, it was possible to measure the thickness of the ice layer—a maximum of 4,500 ft. in Greenland and 14,600 ft. in the Antarctic. A map of Greenland's land outline was drawn, based on the results of these measurements. Using the same method certain parts of the Antarctic were cartographically inferred.

So Arlington Mallery could check the data on the Piri Reis maps with scientific accuracy. His conclusions, which he read to a conference at the University of Georgetown, were that the outlines of Greenland, as drawn by the Turkish admiral, tallied with the land outline established by the French polar expedition. The coastline which prolongs the South American coastline is in reality the Antarctic coastline. Mallery took the trouble to follow the map inch by inch and compare it with the most recent data. The results were surprising. For example, it turned out that the islands which Piri Reis had included off the coast coincide with the mountain tops that exist under the ice today and were discovered by a Norwegian-Swedish-British Antarctic expedition to Queen Maud Land.

Mallery, who continued his comparisons tirelessly, used

a coastal map of the Antarctic that had been made recently. In his opinion, they matched perfectly except in one place—Piri Reis had put in two bays where the new map showed terra firma. Mallery discussed the problem at the Hydrographical Institute. His arguments induced some well-known scholars to make seismic check measurements at this point. Piri Reis's maps were right; "Work carried out to date," says R. P. Linehan, "show that these maps seem to be extremely accurate. And I think," he added, "that further seismic research would prove that they are even more accurate than we assume today."

But this opinion is by no means shared by everyone. The Russians, who collaborated with the western nations in Antarctic research, have advanced other theories. They have reached the conclusion that Piri Reis's drawing does not show the Antarctic, but the southern border of Patagonia and Tierra del Fuego. But even that is puzzling, for these countries were not known until 1520.

We must step carefully where so little agreement prevails. The first thing that is clear is that Piri Reis possessed data about the American continent from the time before the "discovery" by Christopher Columbus. It is conceivable that these data were taken from the medieval Viking epics. But however daring the Vikings were, they still knew only a small part of America and they did not realize that it was a continent. Recently a map dating to 1440 was discovered in Switzerland. On it, at the same height as Scandinavia, Iceland is drawn, then Greenland, and lastly a large island, on which scholars think they can make out the estuaries of the St. Lawrence and the Hudson. The inscription reads: "Discoveries by Bjarni and Leif." According to the Norwegian sagas Bjarni Herjolfsson and Leif Eriksson are supposed to have sailed to the American continent in 986 and 1002 respectively.

So the Vikings alone cannot explain Piri Reis's maps. Yet there are other facts: the Gloreanus map of 1510, which is in the library of Bonn University. In other words, it is older than Piri Reis's maps. It shows not only the exact line of the Atlantic coast of America from Canada to Tierra del Fuego, but also that of the whole length of the Pacific coast.

The historians have not yet solved the mystery of these maps. We must stick to the chronology. First let us take the Russian theory. What Piri Reis drew was not the Antarctic, but Patagonia and Tierra del Fuego. At that time these two countries were unknown. The only sea-faring people who could possibly be supposed to have had this knowledge were the Phoenicians. It is historically proved that they traded along the whole of the west coast of Europe. Did they also venture on the endless expanse of the ocean? It is certain that a tradition telling of a fabulous continent on the other side of the ocean persisted throughout antiquity and into the Middle Ages. Greece's chroniclers speak of a continent called "Antichthone" (i.e. the land of the Antipodes). The priest and scholar Isidor of Seville (560 to 636) is reputed to have said: "There is another continent besides the three known ones. It lies beyond the ocean and the sun is much hotter there than in our region." Then there is the little known epic of the Breton monks who set forth on a dramatic and dangerous crusade to convert to Christianity the people of this cele-brated continent which they had heard about. We know that they put to sea from the coast of Brittany. Did one of their ships reach America?

There are valid arguments in favor of the Phoenician hypothesis, especially the fact that finds with Mediter-ranean characteristics have been made in South and North America. Admittedly, they are controversial, but the idea of the Phoenicians being able to cross the ocean is not fantastic *per se*. They could have accomplished this remarkable feat with their fleet, which was used both for trading and as a naval force. It is more difficult to explain why they should have kept their discovery secret. How-ever, the power of their little country depended solely on their fleet and broadcasting newly discovered trading places would have attracted their competitors to the spot. Later the secret may simply have been lost. We need only think of the Vikings. A couple of centuries after their voyages, Greenland, Newfoundland and Canada had to be "rediscovered."

Now we should like to tackle Mallery's theory. Piri Reis knew the geographical data of Greenland and the Antarctic dating from the period before the glaciation, as heir to a long series of secret traditions. This is where the first question arises. When did this glaciation take place? The Geophysical Year has stimulated research into this problem. In 1957, Dr. J. L. Hough of the University of Illinois, using soundings and Dr. W. D. Hurry of the Carnegie Institute in Washington, using the radio carbon method, have narrowed it down. They say that the period of the present glaciation of the poles began from 6,000 to 15,000 years ago. The experts (particularly Claude Lorius, the glaciologist on the French polar expedition) place the beginning of the glaciation between 9,000 and 10,000 years ago. Apart from that, they agree that a period of deglaciation has just begun. So it seems possible that about ten millennia ago Greenland and the Antarctic had the same shape as they have on Piri Reis's maps. A part of the land masses that are under the ice or submerged today was visible then.

So we could conclude that the knowledge needed to prepare these maps is 10,000 years old.

This conclusion is inevitable, but it contradicts all the classical theories about the evolutionary stages of human cultures and must be accepted with the greatest caution. What do the text-books on prehistory say? They say that 10,000 years was the age of Cromagnon man, who did not know metallurgy, agriculture or stock raising.

But Mallery also has this to say: "At the time when the maps were made, there must have been not only explorers, but also hydrographical specialists, for neither a single explorer nor even a group of explorers can make maps of continents or enormous territories, as apparently happened some thousands of years ago. It can only be done by experienced technicians who are equally conversant with astronomy and the methods of cartography."

Mallery goes even further. He says: "I cannot understand how these maps could have been made without the help of aviation. Moreover, the degrees of longitude are absolutely accurate—something we ourselves were unable to achieve until two centuries ago."

So we ought to undertake a thorough-going revision of our ideas of the history of mankind. What speculations can be made about a highly developed civilization that supposedly lived thousands of years ago?

As a specialist in pre-Columbian America, Mallery was searching for traces of a vanished civilization, which was supposed to have existed on the American continent. He was able to produce abundant evidence, some of which was sensational, especially blast furnaces of great antiquity for treating iron and stones with mysterious inscriptions. They were discovered in the State of Pennsylvania, near Harrisburg. The experts whose advice Mallery sought found similarities with Phoenician and Cretan inscriptions. However that may be, these inscriptions appear to date to a time before the first inscriptions in Mediterranean countries. The use of alphabets had actually already begun there, but this writing which is not a genuine syllabic writing, has 170 signs. So far, it has not been deciphered.

Mallery thinks that it is the writing of an old American culture that is older than the known pre-Columbian Incan, Mayan or Aztec cultures. He assumes that these three preserved some vestiges of the first-named culture. That would explain the mysterious and undatable fortress of Tiahuanaco, many peculiarities of Mayan astronomy and the remarkable legends about earlier bringers of culture. But if there was such a culture on the American continent

10,000 years ago, one would like to know how its geographical lore could have reached Europe.

As we have now broken the bounds of reason, we can give our imagination free rein and ask whether this culture existed not only in America, but throughout the world.

Was it of extraterrestrial origin? At all events, the Piri Reis maps exclude a landing on earth by inhabitants of Venus or other extraterrestrial beings. Surely they would have drawn a complete map of the continent instead of just a map of the coast, equipped as they presumably were with the ultimate in technical aids?

Were they inhabitants of Atlantis or Gondwana, then? But the continental drift goes back more than 10,000 years and in the period in question these continents had long since disappeared, if indeed they ever existed.

We could assume that one branch of the human family tree reached a high level of culture 8,000 to 10,000 years ago and had extensive knowledge of our planet, and that it was completely wiped out from one day to the next by a catastrophe.

Charles H. Hapgood is quite explicit on the subject. It is only a century since the origins of history were backdated and the traces of apparently mythical cultures (Troy, Crete) and even quite unknown ones (the Sumerians and Hittites) discovered.

The American professor says that further research would inevitably lead to the discovery of an advanced culture that existed 10,000 years ago. So the great archaeological find of the century is still to be made.

# 4 The Earth's Scars

Russians, Americans, Chinese, English, French—they all believed that someone had launched an atomic attack, and believed it at the same moment. They all switched on their counter-attack systems at the same moment and the earth burst into flames. Yet the cause was not a politician who had gone mad, but the blind, impartial hand of heaven. A giant meteorite had struck the earth.

That is the way we might end one day, destroyed by heaven.

Gigantic meteorites have struck the earth before. The globe has countless scars of unknown origin. The Barringer crater in Arizona was caused by a 2.5 megaton explosion (twenty-five times the power of the Hiroshima bomb) that happened 50,000 years ago. When the American mining engineer D. M. Barringer decided that the crater was caused by the impact of a giant meteorite, he met with fierce opposition. Scholars attributed it to a volcanic eruption or an explosion of natural gas. Barringer finally convinced his opponents. Today it is assumed that what took place was a collision between the earth and a 10,000 tons object moving at a speed of 25 miles per second. Microscopic iron balls were found near the crater that presumably originated from the condensation of a cloud of iron vapor caused by the impact.

The Barringer crater is not the biggest. The Vredefort crater in South Africa has a volume of 10 cubic kilometers. The projectile apparently broke through the earth's crust and the lava that was ejected filled part of the crater.

There may have been even more disastrous collisions. It is possible that the Sea of Japan, Hudson Bay and the

Weddell Sea, the sea on the southern border of the Atlantic, originated in this way. If that is so, the energy must have been of the astronomical order of $10^{33}$ ergs. In itself this figure does not mean anything, but it corresponds to a quarter of the energy radiated by the sun in 1 second or the 100 per cent transformation of 1,000,000 tons of matter into energy.

There is an objection to such hypotheses. A collision of this violence would have raised the temperature of the atmosphere around our planet to 200°C. The entire surface of the earth would have become sterile. Admittedly, there is no trace of such a sterilization in the known biological history of the globe, but collisions that liberate the energies of a million tons appear to be perfectly possible.

In Canada there are at least a dozen scars with diameters ranging from 1 to 37 miles; they are between 200,000,000 and 500,000,000 years old. In Australia there is the Wolf Creek crater and in the United States a circular crater that forms a lake called Deep Bay, with a diameter of 7½ miles and a depth of 500 ft.

As we can calculate, a projectile of more than 1,000 tons that moves at a high speed would not be slowed down by the atmosphere. A projectile from the solar system could not exceed a speed of 25 miles per second, otherwise it would be hurled out of the system. So a meteorite that hit the earth at a speed of 95 miles per second would have to come from regions beyond the solar system.

The chances are three to one that a meteorite will fall in the sea. The collision would make the ocean evaporate for thousands of miles around. The whole earth would be enveloped day and night in a covering of cloud as thick as Venus's. Colossal tidal waves, caused by submarine earthquakes, would surge over the planet. We can picture such an event in our imagination. Probably it has already happened in the past. A tidal wave like that

57

would be like the Flood described in myths and legends throughout the world.

Consequently, a whole series of cultures could have been destroyed by "the wrath of heaven."

Earth's scars bear witness to two or three catastrophes within a time span of a million years. That is enough to call the classical theory of evolution in question. The traditional theory of the origin of the ice-ages should also be questioned, for the dense clouds composed of steam and dust which formed after the impact of the meteorite must have reflected the solar energy, resulting in a considerable, reduction in the average temperature. The American scientist already mentioned, R. S. Dietz, showed that the Canadian nickel mines at Sudbury originated from the impact of a meteorite. These mines have been worked since 1860. So for over a century men have been extracting cosmic energy, heavenly wealth, without realizing it. The giant meteorite landed 1.7 million years ago. Its mass contained a considerable quantity of nickel. That is startling when we think of the relative proportions of iron and nickel in the small meteorites that land in our own time. Research on the subject is still in progress, but one thing is certain: the origin of the earth must be backdated once again.

This is the most interesting of the many problems thrown up by the earth's scars. Investigation of the moon and observation of Mars show that these planets are strewn with giant meteorites. The earth has been spared this. Admittedly, its atmosphere has made small meteorites burn up, but there seems to be no doubt that the atmosphere could hardly keep meteorites of more than 1,000 tons away from the earth. So we can postulate a magnetic or electro-magnetic shield provided by the electrically charge layers surrounding the earth. However, a shield of this kind would primarily keep away meteors that are rich in magnetic material such as nickel. So how can the impact at Sudbury be explained?

Let us use our imagination. If the earth is the only planet in the solar system on which life flourishes, have "almighty engineers" in outer space taken steps to protect life on earth? Perhaps beings in the Milky Way interfere with the celestial mechanism so that life on this tiny planet can continue and develop.

The second problem concerns the actual phenomenon of the collision. Matter can no longer remain in a gaseous state at the exceptionally high temperatures created. It assumes the fourth state, plasma, i.e. the atoms lose a large part of their electrons. A ball of fire and a circular whirlwind are created. (This would mean that the craters on the moon and on the earth are the fossilized traces of this whirlwind.) The whirlwind tears off the earth's crust and magma spurts out. Then it explodes and the explosion can hurl fragments of the earth into space at a speed of 50 miles per second. No doubt there is still a lot to be discovered, for we do not know very much about the fourth state of matter. But it is possible that fragments of the earth's substance could be shot forth so fast that they escaped from the solar system and carried organic matter into outer space.

Thus fragments that were torn from the earth 1.7 milliard years ago by the Sudbury meteorite may have reached a fertile and hospitable environment somewhere in the universe.

The theory of continental shift supported by contemporary geologists, research into the big craters and investigation of the mechanics of giant meteorites seem to be more compelling than the revelations proclaimed by occultists and the necessity to suppose that unknown cultures existed. Apocalyptic traditions, myths and legends must be reinterpreted. But one thing is clear. The earth's scars prove that the history of our earth and of mankind are irrevocably bound up with the history of the solar system, and indeed of the whole universe. The same cosmic explosion may have wrenched the planet Pluto out of its orbit, when it was a satellite of Neptune, and bombarded the earth at Sudbury. Other disturbances in space may have caused giant meteorites to strike terra firma or land in the ocean, originated glaciations, destroyed cultures and covered the sky with clouds so thick that when they were dispersed one day, men discovered the stars—the stars that they had never seen before so that they knew nothing of the rhythm of days followed by starlit nights. According to a South American tradition, the culture of Tiahuanaco existed *before* the stars. Before the stars? That sounds absurd, if we take it literally. But it is not so absurd if we imagine that in the not too distant past men had seen the cloud cover dissolve and a star-strewn sky sparkling above them for the first time.

It is always claimed that no culture could have developed without the stars, because men would have had no knowledge of the laws of nature and no consciousness of infinity. If this is so, scientific research only began at the moment when the stars became visible again. Perhaps that was the time when our ancestors established a stellar calendar at Stonehenge.

The interactions between the earth, the other planets and almost certainly the whole cosmos should be more important for the life and death of cultures than is generally admitted by the scientific Establishment, which clings religiously to an inner causality, to continuous evolution and a simple dynamic of the "progress" of human history. The idea that such interactions have influenced and still influence on our earth and that this concept can bring about a radical change in human history is a prerequisite for our theory that the disappearance and reappearance of men on this earth has been a constant process.

# 5   Two Fairy-tales Throw Light on our History

The reader will have realized by now that this book does not preach a new religion. We hear no voices. We do not have access to esoteric knowledge.

But as the existence in the remote past of a stage of humanity of which we know nothing cannot be categorically rejected, we can give free rein to our imagination. And so we are going to carry out two exercises in mental acrobatics. We are going to pursue two theories. The first was suggested by the American engineers Walt and Leigh Richmond, the second by the Soviet writer Nikolai D. Rudenko. Two theories or, more accurately, two fairy-tales. We shall call the first one the Fairy-tale of the Solar Wind, the second the Fairy-tale of Phaeton.

Nearly all traditions tell of an ancient world and its destruction by a catastrophe. Of course, this may be simply a myth, but the question remains whether the concept of a humanity that creates myths is not itself a modern myth. Perhaps myths are really garbled versions of actual facts and events. The occultists, who firmly believe that the Golden Age lies behind us, preach their gospel, but their information comes from such mysterious sources that they fail to convince us unfortunate unbelievers.

In addition to the occultists, other theoreticians made a heady brew by mixing the old legends with astronomy, geology, climatology, botany, zoology and anthropology in an attempt to establish the location of the first great culture and explain its development and disappearance. Ignatius Donnelly's book *Atlantis*, which appeared in 1882, had a great success. Making "a mountain of conjectures out of a molehill of facts," the author situated the lost paradise in what is now the Atlantic Ocean. The gods of antiquity were the lords of the lost continent. Like his predecessor Donnolly, the psychoanalyst Velikovski,[1] basing himself on the controversial theory that Venus was originally a comet detached from Jupiter and had twice brushed against the earth, explains Genesis and Exodus, and interprets the Holy Scriptures in terms of a great natural catastrophe.

Surely it should be possible to put forward theories that are equally imaginative, but less improbable? At any rate we are going to try.

Since the beginning of the industrial revolution, the question has frequently been asked whether the men of earlier ages could not have had an advanced technology at their service. "Man did not wait until the twentieth century to exploit the earth," writes Korium Megertchian, a member of the Armenian Geological Institute. In 1968 he discovered the oldest factory in the world at Medzamor. He explains the legends of the priests of fire handed down by the invaders and inhabitants of Medzamor as memories of the workers in a metallurgical industry dating to the third millennium B.C. And these workers, "wearing gloves, their mouths covered with protective filters, were exactly like the operators at Essen, Le Creusot and Donets." Imported ore was treated in this industrial city, which was erected on still earlier levels from which prehistoric workshops are still being excavated. When the journalist Jean Vidal returned from Armenia, where he had collaborated with Megertchian and his colleagues in their researches, he wrote in the review *Science et vie* (July, 1969): "There is so much unknown material still hidden at Medzamor that to draw up a list of the objects found would only produce a provisional balance. But among these finds there was one that took the historians of metallurgy by surprise. It was steel tweezers, several examples of which were taken from layers dating to the beginning

[1] In *Worlds in Collision*, 1959.

of the first millennium B.C. These tweezers, rather like eyebrow tweezers, enable chemists and watchmakers to handle micro-objects which they cannot manipulate by hand."

"Medzamor," he continues, "was founded by the wise men of earlier civilizations. They possessed knowledge they had acquired during a remote age that is unknown to us and deserves to be called 'scientific and industrial prehistory'. The builders of Medzamor had as their masters and architects, astronomers and metallurgists of the Neolithic, whose culture was already scientific. Even before the Sumerian civilization flowered, man lived in an organized society, the structure of which was the same as our own in many respects."

The even earlier finds at Catal Hüyük and Lepenski-Vir (urban cultures dating to about 7000 and 5500 B.C.) had already puzzled the archaeologist James Mellaart when he found copper objects surrounded by slag-metal. For that meant that the men of those days knew how to separate metal from ore and use fire to shape it. Medzamor, which is 600 miles from Catal Hüyük, is the first revelation of a prehistoric technology that was absolutely unsuspected ten years ago.

Traces of a very advanced technique, of an unknown civilization, which perished in a catastrophe? A legitimate question which entails yet another question. What kind of a catastrophe was it? Was it unleashed by god or man? That leads us to the first of our fairy-tales, the Fairy-tale of the Solar Wind.

Once upon a time, 20,000 years ago, there was a great civilization that was passionately interested in the sun. When it disappeared, man, spurred on by vague memories, continued to pray and sacrifice to the sun.

Comparison with our own achievements may give us an idea of the titanic labors they performed. Apart from the comparatively small amounts of energy derived from the atom, our energy comes from the sun, either in fossil form (coal, oil), or in direct form (hydro-electric energy, the product of evaporation). We also make solar batteries which transform the sun's rays into energy. We can imagine more effective methods, for example, the use of thermo-nuclear energy by the fusion of light and heavy nuclei. And an attempt could be made to harness the solar wind. This consists of atoms of solar matter which escape and strike our globe. It is thought that this wind causes the aurora borealis and also the formation of the electrical layers in the atmosphere. If it was possible to create a short-circuit between the electrified layers in the upper atmosphere and the sun, a vast, inexhaustible source of energy would be captured. How could the atmosphere be made conductive? A laser beam, which would have an effect similar to lightning, could produce this phenomenon.

Twenty thousand years ago, a scientifically and technically oriented civilization had the idea of exploiting the solar wind. Enormous insulators shaped like pyramids were built in many parts of the world. Apparatuses which sent forth laser beams were installed on their summits. (Much later these instruments must have haunted the memory of surviving generations. For no apparent reason, the men of later cultural ages built pyramids and often placed flashing stones encased in metal on their summits.)

The experiment was carried out, but the power snatched from the sun annihilated the world, whose inhabitants saw "the sky roll up like a parchment scroll and the moon become like blood."

The enormous insulators were destroyed. Much later, in the twentieth century of our era, tectites were discovered in the places where they had once stood in Africa, Australia and Egypt. Tectites are a kind of glass which has been exposed to exceptionally high temperatures and bombarded by particles of high energy.

Did any of these scholars and technicians survive? Perhaps some of them had taken shelter in deep caves;

perhaps others were travelling in space? The situation after the great catastrophe was disastrous both geologically (collapsed or submerged continents) and biologically. The bombardment from the atmosphere had created a large amount of radioactive carbon. Breathed in by animals and man, it must have led to mutations and the appearance of fantastic hybrids. These centaurs, satyrs and bird-men were to haunt men's memories for a long time, right down to oriental and classical antiquity.

The survivors had to face a serious technical problem. How were they to eliminate the carbon 14? They hit on the idea of arranging a gigantic washing of the atmosphere by artificial rainfall, in order to preserve the human being and animal species which had not been mutated.

Our interpretation is an attempt to decipher tradition without resorting to the occult. Are we on the right track? We do not know, but we hope that one day a genius with the unswerving faith of a Schliemann, the discoverer of Troy, and the brilliance of a Darwin, will assemble the scattered elements of the truth and write the prehistory of our planet.

If we situate the great catastrophe 20,000 years back in time, that takes into account the anomalies which occur in carbon 14 dating. When the process first appeared, scholars thought they could safely assume that archaeology would become an exact science. The method enables us to fix dates up to 50,000 years. Yet strangely enough there are no finds that can be placed in the period between 20,000 and 25,000 B.C., although we have finds from before and after those dates. So far no explanation of this phenomenon has been found. It seems feasible that an event that modified the concentration of carbon 14 in the atmosphere took place in those days.

It is very likely that the legends which refer to beings who were half-man, half-beast, were based on fact. Objection: no such bones have been found. Answer: they have, but the archaeologists think that they have found a man buried together with an animal in graves devoted to some totemic religion.

Our fairy-tale proposes to use methods borrowed from physics in an attempt to establish the date of the putative great catastrophe. If it was due to a short-circuit in the earth's atmosphere, the short-circuit would undoubtedly have disturbed the magnetic field and perhaps even displaced the magnetic poles. This is something which requires more detailed investigation.

The field of tectites could help to identify the source of the catastrophe. Examination of the nuclear composition of tectites shows that they did not travel in space for long. So they must have been formed either on the earth or on the moon. It has been proved that they travelled through the atmosphere at a great speed, which also indicates that they came from the moon or rose from the earth through some explosive kind of cataclysm. We might find traces of this cataclysm in the form of trajectories in certain minerals through which particles with high energy have passed. It only needs scientific circles to take the theory of a great catastrophe seriously for physical investigation to be undertaken. Perhaps then we should obtain information which would completely upset our ideas of the history of mankind.

Lastly, our story shows that the examination of mythology as a basis for actual research is still in its infancy. The myths that deal with catastrophes must be reinterpreted from this point of view, especially the legends which tell us about fire from heaven and mention fabulous creatures.

Has racialism influenced research into man's origin? The question arises since the publication of the celebrated theory of Sheikh Anta Diop, which traces the culture of ancient Egypt back to a negro civilization. In *Antériorité des civilisations nègres*. Anta Diop writes: "On the basis of the results of archaeological excavations, especially those made by Dr. Leakey in East Africa, we can push the first tentative examples of mankind further back into the night of time nearly every six months. Nevertheless, we will accept that *homo sapiens* lived approximately 40,000 years ago in the Upper Palaeolithic. This first type of man, who belonged to the lower levels of the Aurignacian, was probably morphologically close to the black type of modern man. If we are completely objective, we cannot help admitting that the first *homo sapiens* was a negroid and that the other races, the white and yellow came later, as the result of differentiations, the physical causes of which are not yet known to science. Everything points to the fact that the negroes predominated in prehistoric times. Even in historical times they still predominated in the field of civilization and military and technological matters."

According to this writer our ancestors were black. Did they live in a harmonious synthesis of science and religion? Did they endow their destiny with a higher meaning? What faith sustained them when the sun exploded? If the Bible relays a distant echo of their tragedy, it was these thieves of the sun who first spoke the sublime words: "The Lord giveth, the Lord has taken away, blessed be the name of the Lord."

And this is the Fairy-tale of Phaeton.

It also reflects an interruption in evolution, but in this case the catastrophe was not unleashed by man. "The key to the door which separates us from inner nature has been rusty since the Flood," says the writer Gustav Meyrink. In the opinion of the Ukrainian Nikolai D. Rudenko, this is not our fault, but that of the intelligences on the planet Phaeton. And now that they can no longer do us any harm, we shall win. Our earlier civilizations were technically highly developed. They were destroyed by the explosion of Phaeton, but henceforth such apocalypses no longer threaten us. Has more than one end of the world taken place? At all events, there will be no more. Our civilization is immortal. At least we ourselves can decide if there are to be ends of the world in the future.

In 1959, Czechoslovakian astronomers succeeded in establishing the origin of a meteorite which had fallen in that country. The cosmic projectile came from space, between Mars and Jupiter. It was one of the thousands of planetoids which had fallen in this region since the beginning of the nineteenth century. They thought that it was a tiny fragment of the planet Phaeton, which disappeared from the sky in the remote past. When? Rudenko thinks in terms of some tens of thousands of years. The Russian astronomer W. G. Fessenkov pushes the date when Phaeton exploded a good deal further back. If this planet was inhabited, were the Akpallus, the strange fish- or frogmen mentioned by the Babylonian Berosos (fourth/third century B.C.), survivors who travelled through space, visited the earth and imparted the rudiments of knowledge to the men on the shores of the Persian Gulf? And if clusters of fragments of Phaeton rained down on earth on several occasions, might they not have destroyed flourishing cultures each time they did so? Here cosmo-history is taking the place of history. Rudenko sticks to this dream in the book which he calls a *Cosmic Fairy-tale*. (In this half-novel, half-essay, students who examine the problems raised by such a cosmo-history are arrested by the police for trying to create a new religion.)

To this visionary, Jupiter is the biological center of the solar system, in which life has assumed the most perfect forms. The beings on Phaeton occupied an intermediate place in the hierarchy between the inhabitants of Jupiter and earthmen. Through this indirect contact, belief in the existence of a God was born. But Solon, the Greek law-giver, said: "Phaeton, son of the Sun, could not master the chariot of the Sun; he burnt everything on earth and then perished. He was a victim of the fire. He fell to the earth in flames."

And in the *Chilam Balam*, a Mayan collection of myths and chronicles, it says: "The earth quaked. And a rain of fire, ashes and rocks fell. And the waters rose and clashed with each other. And in a second the annihilation took place."

Why did man, who is undoubtedly several millions of years old, only build a great culture in quite recent times? Because it is only a few thousands of years since the falls of debris from Phaeton ceased. Now it only reaches us in the form of dust, tons of it every year, and perhaps it still contains fossilized traces of life. These are the last ghostly visits from the dead planet, from which came the being who formed us and who worshipped the "great brains" of Jupiter.

Thus Phaeton brought to the earth reason, which is the source and protection of life, and we preserve in our minds an atavistic memory which fills us with fear at the sight of shooting stars and makes us direct our prayers to the heavenly powers. In our subconscious we believe that life and spirit are preserved in the constellations.

Today, like the former inhabitants of Phaeton, we possess a power which could blow up our own planet if unleashed. "I write this fairy-tale," says Rudenko, "so that my sons can live in peace and so that we do not commit the same error as the being on Phaeton. So that the heavenly flame, the mastered fire of the sky, does not destroy us in our turn, so that we too do not float away into eternity in clouds of dust."

In recounting these fantastic tales, it is not our intention to try to impose on our readers theories which are far from complete. We only want to show that there are different ideas about the prehistory of mankind.

# PART TWO

Reveries about the Great Language

The Music of the Spof Hell

# 1 The Music of the Giants' Ballet

In the fifth century A.D., Aurelius Ambrosius, successor of Vortigern, wished to erect a monument in memory of his men who had been massacred by the Saxons. He consulted Merlin, the magician, who is honored in Celtic mythology, and Merlin said: "If it is really your wish to honor the burial place of these men by a work that will defy the centuries, then have the Dance of the Giants from Killaraus, a mountain in Ireland, brought here. There is a monument of stones there and today no one would be strong enough to erect one like it, not even if he were wondrous wise. For the stones are enormous, and never did man see stones radiate such power or conceal such a mystery..."

Aurelius sent forth his army. The soldiers were unable to shift the stones and steal the petrified Dance of the Giants. Then Merlin spoke some magic words and the stones grew light, so that they could easily be moved to the coast, where they were loaded on to ships and brought to Stonehenge on Salisbury Plain, "where they shall remain for ever."

That is what we read in that fantastic book, the *History of the Kings of Britain*, written in 1140 by Geoffrey of Monmouth. It is the first description of this sandstone and limestone group, the most astonishing megalithic monument extant. For 500 years, Geoffrey of Monmouth's legend was considered to be true. In 1620, King James I sent the architect Inigo Jones to investigate Stonehenge. He thought it was a Roman temple. The first man to examine Stonehenge thoroughly was John Aubrey, a fervent admirer of the antique and thief of precious relics, who was responsible for gossipy details about Shake-

73

speare in his *Brief Lives*. He made the first topographical discoveries, noticed the arrangement of the strange holes, about which we shall have more to say, and that the stones were placed in concentric circles. Aubrey thought that Stonehenge was of Druidic origin. Dr. Stukely, another lover of the antique and friend of Isaac Newton in his youth, came to the same conclusion a century later.

Systematic excavation began in 1801. Cunnington dug in the center and buried a bottle of port for later archaeologists. Exactly a hundred years later, Professor Gowland found eighty stone axes and hammers under the Roman deposits. They proved that the Dance of the Giants was several thousand years old. In 1950, Aubrey's holes were dated to 1848 B.C. by the carbon 14 method.

What did this complicated neolithic construction look like? There is an outer circumference with a diameter of 115 yards, demarcated by a ditch with internal and external ramps. There is only one break in the ditch to allow for the entrance. Just inside the outer circumference, there is a concentric circle of 56 holes, known as the Aubrey holes. Inscribed within this circle and perpendicular to the entrance there is a rectangle marked at its four corners by stones, only two of which remain. Then there is a circle with a diameter of about 100 ft. made up of 30 stones, each weighing 25 tons, all of them joined by lintels so that they form a series of dolmens. There is a circle of 59 stones and a horseshoe facing the entrance made up of 10 blocks, each weighing 50 tons and connected by horizontal lintels so that they form 5 dolmens. There are also a horseshoe with 19 stones, 3 monoliths or menhirs, one in the center, the other at the entrance and the third outside the ditch in the middle of the avenue leading up to the monument.

Lastly, there are two circles with 30 and 29 holes respectively. They are almost invisible on the ground and partly conjectural, and are situated between the Aubrey holes and the 30 stones weighing 25 tons.

\*     \*     \*

Gerald S. Hawkins, Professor of Astronomy at Boston University, was attached to an experimental missile base in south-west England, at Larkhill, not far from Stonehenge. There he was told that if one stood in the middle of the monument on the morning of the solstice, the sun rose over the Heel Stone and he checked that this was so with his own eyes. Then the astronomer turned archaeologist. His investigations showed that these alignments seemed to form a complicated astronomical observatory. A preliminary examination showed him that there were hundreds of possible alignments. How could one recognize which were the most important? Hawkins fed a computer with the known information about the stones of Stonehenge and the key positions (risings, settings, culminations) of the most important heavenly bodies—the sun, moon, planets and stars.

The computer told him what it saw in the section of the sky between individual stones on specific dates. The result was surprising.

The builders of Stonehenge did not seem to have been interested in the constellation of the planets and stars, but only in that of the sun and the moon. The tables prepared by Hawkins leave no doubt about that. The computer had explained the function of the stone block. But there were cavities at Stonehenge, in addition to the stone blocks. The 56 Aubrey holes, then 30 holes, 29 holes, 56 holes, 30 holes, 29 holes. What did these figures mean? Once the problem had been put, it was easy to solve. Hawkins remembered the "Metonic year." The Greek astronomer Meton observed that every 19 years the full moon fell on the same date in the solar calendar and the eclipses followed the same cycle. Actually, it was not nineteen years, but eighteen point six one, that had to be taken into account when preparing a calendar. If the calendar was constantly rounded off to eighteen or nineteen years, it would soon become noticeable. But if a larger cycle is formed from the smaller Metonic cycle, which is based now on eighteen, now on nineteen years, then dates that are valid for centuries are arrived at. The most convenient approximation, as one can easily calculate—is a larger cycle of 19 + 19 + 18. This gives 56, the exact number of the holes discovered by Aubrey in the seventeenth century. Hawkins, still not satisfied with this discovery, postulated that the Aubrey circle, in conjunction with the megaliths, should have made possible the prediction of the eclipses. The dates of the eclipses that happened during the erection of Stonehenge were calculated. The computer was put to work again. And again the results were positive. A system of stones arranged along the Aubrey circle would make it possible to predict the years in which the eclipses of the sun fell due. What about the days? The lunar month has 29.53 days. So two lunar months give a round figure of 59 days. The 30 holes and 29 holes cropped up again. But yet another circle exists, although we have not mentioned it before, because it is almost entirely conjectural. It is assumed to have had 59 blue stones. Finally, Hawkins succeeded in working out not only the exact dates of the eclipses that occurred when Stonehenge was being built, but also in calculating the date of our moveable Christian holiday of Easter, which, as is well known, goes back to an ancient heathen custom. In other words, Stonehenge is not only an observatory, but a stone calendar as well.

To the best of our knowledge, no one has yet refuted Hawkins' theory. In any case, according to the law of probabilities, the chance of these remarkable stone alignments being explained as a purely coincidental concatenation of circumstances is one in ten million. However, the mystery of Stonehenge is still not solved.

The stone blocks that make up the monument do not come from the ground immediately beneath them. The blue stones, weighing about 5 tons apiece, were brought from a quarry 250 miles away. They had to be transported by sea and land, including the crossing of rivers. How was it done? Other blocks weigh 25 and 50 tons.

The quarries from which they come are situated nearer Stonehenge, but the stones had to be quarried, transported and dressed. All the stones have been worked by human hands. Then they had to be erected. And the lintels, or capstones, had to be laid across them. And it all had to be done to the nearest inch, if we accept the astronomical purpose of Stonehenge proposed by Hawkins. Even today such an undertaking would not be easy, quite apart from the theoretical calculations requiring a knowledge of mathematical, physical and mechanical laws.

Today it is generally accepted that Stonehenge was erected in stages between 2000 and 1700 B.C. Yet prehistoric scholars claim that the men who inhabited the Anglo-Saxon islands at the time were Stone Age men who were beginning to practice agriculture and raise cattle. They were culturally far less advanced than the civilizations that evolved at the same time in the Mediterranean. Scholars have tried to imagine the construction of Stonehenge with the primitive means that would have been at their disposal. We find this conclusion difficult to accept. Millions of working days would have been needed, i.e. whole generations would have had to work on this monument. Yet Stonehenge is only part of an extensive complex. Within a radius of about twelve miles, there are more cromlechs, as these stone circles are called, many of them on a vast scale, such as Avebury, the biggest known cromlech, with a diameter of 365 yards. In addition, there are holes arranged in circles in which the remains of wood were found; a concentrically arranged monument called the Sanctuary; giant tumuli; a right angle surrounded by a ditch 2,800 yards long and 90 yards wide; an artificial mound with 500,000 cubic yards of earth; a gigantic circle with a diameter of 450 yards; a funnel-shaped hole 100 yards deep and streets as broad as motorways. . .

Such prehistoric places of worship, called megaliths, are found in every continent in the world. Scholars have tried to explain them as tombs. It is true that there are many graves underneath them, and it is also true that ashes and bones have been found at Stonehenge between the cromlechs and the other upright blocks of stone. There are also cemeteries near churches, but the churches are not tombs.

The megaliths are distributed in a strange way. They exhibit similar characteristics and they are found in separate groups which have no connection with each other and are never far from the coast. They were all apparently erected in the first half of the second millennium B.C. and none of them has left any traces except the legends which are still current in our own day.

Hawkins noticed something else, too. Stonehenge is situated in the part of the northern hemisphere where the azimuths of the sun and the moon form an angle of 90° at their maximum declination. The symmetrical site in the southern hemisphere would have been the Falkland Islands and the Straits of Megellan. Could the builders of Stonehenge calculate degrees of latitude and longitude?

It all looks as if "missionaries" had left some unknown center, bringing ideas and techniques with them, and travelled round the world, mostly by sea. These "propagandists" would have made contact with certain peoples, but not with others. That would explain why there are "gaps" or zones where megaliths are sparsely distributed, and why some groups of megaliths are quite isolated. It would also explain how and why the megalithic monuments were superimposed on the Neolithic culture. And it would clarify the legends which attributed the erection of these great stone tombs to supernatural beings. Lastly, we should know why men who were capable of putting 100-ton blocks upright and topping them with equally heavy cross-stones have left us no other trace of their extraordinary ability. The Irish sagas tell of giants from the sea who were farmers and builders. Greek literature has references to the Hyperboreans, the fabulous people from the far north, and to their round temples in which

Apollo, the sun god, was supposed to appear every 19 years. In fact, everything we know about the stone tombs, especially about the lay-out of Stonehenge which is the most completely preserved and has been most thoroughly investigated, makes us suspect the influence of a culture in prehistoric times that we know nothing about. Today there is no doubt that this complicated monument was erected on the basis of well-founded scientific knowledge.

Philologists have recognized that we must attribute another essential function to the language of primitive peoples, over and above the ability to communicate. It has been established that among the Dogon, a tribe in south-west Nigeria, the word *so,* which designates language, also means the faculty which distinguishes men from animals, the language of one human group which differs from that of another, the word, and conversation. Among primitive peoples everywhere, the word is synonymous with action and designates the various stages of creation. The language of the Dogon is based on a complete identification of personal speech with the life of the community.

In her book *Le Langage, cet inconnu,* Julia Joyaux tells the following Melanesian legend: the god Gomawe met two men who could not answer his questions; indeed they could not speak at all. The god assumed that this was because their bodies were empty, so he took two rats and tore out their entrails. Then he cut open the stomachs of the two men and transplanted the heart, liver and entrails of the rats into them. At once the men began to speak. "What is your stomach?" asked one of them. And that means: "What is your language?" Thus a connection between the origin of language and the intestines is established in this legend.

Language is conceived as material reality. The word "throw" means the same as to shoot an arrow. We must

79

also bear in mind that the word which reproduces a thought existed long before the visceral language just mentioned. There is a primordial word created by God. The Bambara, a Sudanese negro tribe, for example, believe that in a very remote golden age men without voices lived. In their view, this did not imply a lack of ability to communicate, because at one time knowledge and information could be transmitted without being expressed in speech.

Lastly, very subtle and detailed theories about the graphic correlations of words have been observed among many primitive societies. In vanished cultures, the graphic systems show that a clear division was made in language between the sign and the thing represented. This presumes a highly developed symbolism. Mayan writing, which is still undeciphered, appears to go back to religious cults and also to a whole science based on a cyclical concept of time. The Easter Island writing, also undeciphered, suggests the repertory of a religious singer. 1,500 to 2,000 combinations can be made from the 120 signs. Some of these signs—men, heads, arms, animals, objects, plants and geometrical patterns—are genuine images, a woman being represented by a flower, for example.

These and many other facts lead to the conclusion that the language of prehistoric times was already highly developed.

Like other megalithic structures, Stonehenge is evidence of a culture that had extensive mathematical knowledge and formulated myths about the origin of the universe. This raises the question of what language was spoken in this culture. We must assume that writing existed. For how could such difficult calculations have been made without writing?

Why has nothing come down to us? Perhaps the traces have been dispersed with the passage of the centuries. Or perhaps the master-builders—they may have come from Crete—inscribed their signs on a material that has perished. Yet clay tablets were already used as writing materials at that time. Did the master-builders belong to a priesthood who did not speak, but worked through an unknown telepathic medium? Or did they register their thoughts on specially prepared glasses in a way that later generations could not perceive? Or did the masters keep the words which enabled them to build such massive structures secret from the common people?

The fact remains that to erect these edifices another writing, however primitive it was, a general medium of communication, must have existed side by side with the writing of the masters and has now been lost.

For the people of antiquity, written language was only a substitute for the true knowledge that was inscribed in the higher regions of the spirit. Thus, according to Plato, if the father of the universe were discovered, it would be impossible to make everyone recognize him. The philosopher says that books are like portraits; they look alive, but cannot answer when you ask them a question.

Does this mean that Stonehenge, the monument of a vanished great culture, originated without the help of any visible graphic signs of communication? Is every script only a system of signs for the uninitiated, a by-product of knowledge, a vehicle bringing information to the common people? Yet some kind of visible script was indispensable for the smooth running of a large-scale building site such as Stonehenge.

The knotted cords called *quipus* found in Peru gives us another idea. They could have transmitted figures and other technical data. Similar cords were found in the Netherlands. According to magic tradition, they could "bind or free the wind." If such a writing was used during the erection of Stonehenge, the damp earth in the neighborhood of Salisbury must have destroyed all traces of it.

Here is another theory. There might have been a script that was too large or too small to have been read. Microdots like those used by spies or gigantic signs imprinted on the countryside.

Did the know-how exist without men being able to

communicate it to others? Shall we discover the remains of a lost writing one day and so be able to reconstruct the "Great Primordial Language"?

The Greek historian Herodotus mentions an Egyptian king who had two of his children brought up without any contact with any kind of language. The first word the children finally spoke meant bread. They spoke the word in the language of Phrygia, a region in modern Asia Minor. From this, the king concluded that the Phrygian language was older than Egyptian and had been given to men ready-made, as it were.

People have puzzled about the origin of language from prehistoric times, from the legendary king of Egypt to the French structuralist Lévi-Strauss, who claims that language could only have appeared suddenly, that mankind passed without transition from a stage where nothing had a meaning to another stage when everything had a meaning.

Was there then, for all men, some great original language, through which, by the original word, things revealed their true nature, their real name and their function in the universal harmony?

And was the Dance of the Giants of Stonehenge danced to the music of this "Great Language."

## 2 The Hundredth Name of the Lord

"A Jew," said the writer Gustav Meyrink, "is someone who is circumcised, knows why he is and knows the Name in all its forms. The Lord our God has ninety-names which are accessible to the normal human understanding; they correspond to ninety-nine qualities. He is righteous, merciful, omnipotent, etc. But he has a hundredth name which shines in the heavens. The man who learns it becomes a superman. He unites in himself infinite thoughts and infinite power. He is the master of this name. A long chain of masters of the name, says Israel Bar Shem, link the centuries with the original Revelation, from the immortal Melchisedek to our own days."

The Jewish mystic Eleasar of Worms said that the name was inscribed on a sword and whenever the Wandering Jew sees this sword, he has to set off on his travels again.

In a story by the Argentinian writer Jorge Luis Borges (*The Divine Inscription*), the magician Tzinacan, priest in charge of sacrifices on the pyramid of Qaholom, is shut in a deep dungeon because he will not betray the hiding place of the treasure to the Spaniards. A jaguar is waiting on the other side of the wall to devour him. Tzinacan seeks the name, the formula of eternity. God wrote it down on the first day of creation. "He wrote it down in such a way that it would reach distant generations and so that chance could not change it. No one knows where he wrote it, nor in what letters, but we are certain that it continues to exist in its hiding-place and that one day a chosen spirit shall read it. I reflected that as always we stood at the end of time and that the privilege of seeing this writing fell to me because of my destiny, as the last priest of the god. The fact that I was shut up in a prison did not deprive me of this hope; perhaps I had seen the inscription of Qaholom thousands of times and only needed to understand it . . . As I wrestled with myself like this, I remembered that the jaguar is one of the attributes of the god." And as Tzinacan dies, indifferent to himself and his end, it is on the wild beast's coat that he deciphers "the fiery drawings of the universe."

Primitive, gnostic and cabbalistic traditions all teach that there is one supreme name which is the key to everything. They also teach that every thing and every creature has its true name which contains and expresses its real nature, situation and role in the universal harmony. This concept constantly appears in the classical cultures. The true name of Rome was kept secret and according to legend Carthage was destroyed once the Romans had learnt its hidden name through treachery.

Among the so-called primitive peoples, language is a substance and material power; it is not understood as an abstraction, but as an element of the body and of nature. Just as mind and matter, language and reality, the signified and the signifying interpenetrate in the unity of the inner and outer worlds, most magical systems are based on an interpretation of the word as an effective, acting power. There are secret words which are too potent to be used by the uninitiated; there are bans on certain words; some words are instruments for conjuring up or driving out devils. In the Akkadian language, "to be" and "to name" are synonymous.

In his famous book, *The Golden Bough*, Sir James George Frazer tells us that among many primitive peoples a man's name, as well as the hair, nails or any other part of the body, can be used as a means to cast a spell on that person. To the American Indian, his name is a part of his body. If someone defaces his name, he is making an attempt on his life.

Julia Joyaux, in the book already quoted, *Le Langage, cet inconnu,* remarks: "The name may not be pronounced, because the act of materialization by speaking it can betray the typical qualities of the person who bears it and so makes him vulnerable to his enemies." When the Eskimos grow old, they are given a new name. The Celts considered their names as synonymous with 'soul' and 'breath'. In Australia and among other peoples, the father did not tell his child his real name, which was known only to a few people, until he took part in the ceremony during which adolescents were received into adult society. In Australia one *forgets* names; people are called 'brother, cousin or nephew'. The Egyptians had two names: the small one which was used publicly and the large one which was kept secret. Similar rites and customs connected with proper names have been preserved among the Kroo, a negro tribe in the Sudan, among tribes on the Ivory Coast, in the Senegal region, in the Philippines, in the Buru Islands (Indonesia) and the island of Chiloé off the south coast of Chile. The Egyptian god Ra complains when he is bitten by a snake: "I am he who has many names and many shapes. . . . My father and mother told me my name; it has been concealed in my body since my birth, so that no one can bewitch me." But finally he reveals his name to Isis, who becomes omnipotent as a result. Words that denote degrees of relationship are also taboo. Among the Kaffirs, women are forbidden to pronounce the names of their husbands and fathers-in-law. In this connection, Frazer recalls that in classical times Ionian women never called their husbands by their names and that no one dared name a father or a daughter while the rites of Ceres were being observed at Rome.

The names of the dead are also taboo. This custom was observed by a people in the Caucasus. Frazer also noticed it among Australian aborigines. In the language of the Paraguayan Abipon Indians new words were introduced every year, for they removed all words resembling the names of the dead and replaced them by others. This procedure makes history and legends impossible. Language is no longer the guardian of the past, because it changes constantly.

The names of kings, saints, gods and many generic names are also taboo. In the last-named case, this applied particularly to the names of animals and plants that were considered dangerous. Anyone who pronounced them put himself in danger. Thus in the Slavic languages, the word for "bear" was replaced by an innocuous word whose root is "honey". The evil bear is called by a euphemistic name.

Many magic practices are based on the belief that words possess a concrete and effective reality. This is the basis of prayers and magic formulas intended to bring about beneficient results such as rain for the fields and good harvests.

Our civilization has established a dichotomy between mind and matter, between language and reality. This dualistic view of life makes us consider language as a separate function and linguistics as a science on its own. An etymologist like Franz Boas goes so far that he denies any relationship between a people's language and its culture. But in the view of Bronislaw Malinowski, there is not only a relationship between language and the cultural conditions under which it was created, but also, in the case of magic, a relationship between the word, the breath, the tone, the mental attitude, the moment, the place and the receptivity of the assembly in which the magic spoken to a rhythmical accompaniment, and the effect that it sought. We know very little about the powers of sound that were known to the "magic" cultures. So far we have not made a systematic study of breath and its articulation as a "machine", as a means for acting on the psychic processes. It may be that linguistics is only a science of externals and that there is a science of the essence of speech that we shall only discover or rediscover one day in the future.

The idea that there are "master words" which are a key to the understanding of reality is expressed in varying degrees in "primitive" mentalities and gnostic philosophies. Each thing, each being, has its mysterious name, which is recorded in the register of absolute knowledge. God *named* his creation in a language which the elect will be summoned to know. "Very few men," said the gnostic, "may posses this knowledge, one in a thousand, two in ten thousand." (Basilides, Irenaeus, *Adversus haereses*.) Simon the Magus begins his great revelation as follows: "This is the writing about the revelation of the Voice and the Name which came from the Thought and the great eternal Power. That is why it is sealed, hidden, enclosed in the place where the root of the All grows."

So according to tradition, there was a language in which names were not symbols for things, but the expression *and* the reality of the ultimate structure of things. Consequently, our own language is only a confused reminiscence of this divine original language. Sometimes a word seems to be connected with its divine root. Its illuminating ambivalence or its complex numerical content seems to suggest a link with the primordial truths. For example, the word "phos" in Greek means "man" or "light," depending on the accentuation, and among the Christian gnostic sects in the Roman Empire, members used gems engraved with the magic word *Abraxas* or *Abrasax* as recognition signals. In his book *Les Gnostiques,* Serge Hutin writes: "By adding up the respective numerical values of this word— in classical Greek, letters were represented by numbers— we get 365. This is also the number symbolic of Mithra, the god of light, and at the same time corresponds to the number of circles that the sun seems to describe and to the belief of the Gnostic Basilides's adherents that there were 365 heavens or universes." So every word in the "true language" was knowledge and magic, i.e. the revelation of the structure of the things named and absolute power over that thing.

In his celebrated book *Le Mystère des Cathédrales* (1926), Fulcanelli said that the great mediaeval sacred edifices are books in stone which teach the science of alchemy and contain the same positive truth, the same scientific basis, as the Egyptian pyramids, the Greek temples, the Roman catacombs and the Byzantine basilicas. Fulcanelli proposes a new interpretation of the term "Gothic art" an interpretation based on the idea that an original language existed.

"Some acute authors, struck by the similarity between 'Gothic' and 'geotic,' have thought that there must be a connection between Gothic art and the geotic art, or magic.

"In my opinion, Gothic art (*art gothique*) is only an orthographic deformation of the word *argotique,* which is a perfect homophone, in accordance with the phonetic law which is governed by the traditional cabbala in all languages and completely disregards orthography. The cathedral is a work of *art goth* or *argot*. Now dictionaries define *argot* as 'a language used by people who wish to communicate with each other without being understood by third parties.' In other words, argot is a spoken cabbala. Those who use argot are the descendants of the argo-nauts, who manned the ship *Argo* and spoke the argotic language, as they made for the fortunate shores of Colchis to capture the famous Golden Fleece there.

"Lastly, I should mention that argot is one of the forms of speech derived from the language of the birds, the mother of all other languages, the language of the philosophers. Jesus revealed it to his disciples when he sent them his spirit, the Holy Ghost. It is the tongue that reveals the mystery of things and discloses the most hidden truths. The ancient Incas called it the 'language of the court,' because it was known to the 'diplomats,' on whom it conferred both sacred and profane knowledge. In the Middle Ages, it was called 'Gay Wisdom,' 'Language of the Gods' or 'the Divine Bottle.' Tradition has it that men spoke it before the building of the tower of Babel."

What are we to make of all the constantly recurring and widespread traditions? We do not wish to overrate them, but we can ask if there is not a reasonable basis for research in this direction. All the indications are that the origin of language does merely go back to the age of Neanderthal man. Even structuralist anthropology assumes that it appeared suddenly. "Language can only have been born spontaneously" (Lévi-Strauss). Edward Sapir considers that language was "formally complete" from the beginning and that language has existed since man existed. For Leroi-Gourhan, the most ancient traces of a language and graphic symbols go back to the end of the Mousterian and become abundant about 35,000 years B.C. He thinks that there was no prehistory of language, but that it was so to speak "given" and "eternal." So we begin to ask ourselves whether the Neanderthal man whom we looked on as our ancestor was not the product of interbreeding, co-existing with an infinitely older *homo habilis* 50,000 years ago. The American historian Alexander Marshak has reported the discovery of many signs on pebbles revealing traces of palaeolithic mathematics. These signs apparently form a lunar calendar that is 35,000 years old. The establishment of such a calendar implies the existence of advanced mathematical knowledge or at least of records of periodicity. If all this was the remains of a vanished culture older than the Neanderthal culture, we may have discovered the traces of a great primordial language. We could also imagine a cave age in which the survivors of an unknown culture and Neanderthal men co-existed, just as in this space age NASA engineers co-exist with Coghi Indians.

Lastly, we have only just begun to decipher ancient languages by computer—languages apparently as complex as Sanskrit and ancient Egyptian. If they were deciphered, they might hold many surprises in store for us.

"The idea that there was a time when all civilized men spoke the same language is by no means confined to Genesis," writes the biologist Lincoln Barnett. "It is found in ancient Egypt and in old Hindu and Buddhist scriptures. In the sixteenth century, the idea was seriously studied by several European philosophers." When we plunge into the abyss of time, we find that the age of man and his civilizations is constantly receding. Twentieth-century philosophers could usefully reconsider this hypothesis by starting further back, in antediluvian times. Then they would have to take the following questions into account. If there was a primordial language, in what form was it preserved and transmitted? We think of clay tablets, of inscriptions on wood or stone. But what if this crude visible writing was used only by societies which succeeded a civilization that had been far more advanced than they were? If the idea of transmitting a secret to initiates is linked with the idea of newly discovered superior knowledge, we can imagine that there was a form of writing that was inaccessible to the public. Today we can record knowledge invisibly, on records, tapes and microfilms. Perhaps one day we shall discover a secret script that is written on stones in the ground or even in ourselves. Even if it was a visible script, we must not forget that all the books in the classical world stored in the libraries of Rhodes, Carthage, Alexandria and elsewhere were destroyed and that less than one per cent of Greek and Roman literature has come down to us.

The remains of past genius are buried in the earth. If further progress is made in the deciphering of unknown languages, mainly with the help of computers, the existence of a writing based on mathematical abstractions will pose insoluble problems. Our archaeological and linguistic studies have always been directed at civilizations less advanced than our own. Otherwise we should often come up against words and expressions that we found inexplicable, just like a nineteenth-century schoolboy with the problem of translating the words laser and transistor in his Latin prose.

The analysis of magic writing might open up another door to the hypothetical Great Language. After the English archaeologist S. F. Hood had studied tablets found at the prehistoric site of Tartaria, in Roumania, he established correlations with Crete, Iraq, Egypt and the Balkan countries. It seems that a single system of magic signs was used more than 6,000 years ago. For example, N. Vlassa, of the Museum at Cluj, has discovered, among remains that probably came from an altar, tablets with signs similar to those found at Vinca, near Belgrade, Tordos, in Roumania, at Troy and on the island of Melos in the Aegean. Hood thinks that this single system of notations originated in Iraq and spread from there. Scholars have not even begun to decipher the magic writings. The various esoteric interpretations are quite unsatisfactory. Many magic alphabets have come down to us and A. E. Waite has published some of them. Yet fundamentally they remain a mystery to us. Mostly they consist of signs more complex than Chinese ideograms. One thing about them that has struck us is that they often look remarkably like diagrams of printed circuits. We know that the printed circuits in transistors, for example, are electronic circuits recorded with inks that are resistant, conductive and magnetic. The following idea may seem far-fetched. Could special lines drawn on parchment have been the instruments of telecommunication or receptacles of energy? At all events, we ought to examine magic writing much more thoroughly.

David Kahn, one of the most important American specialists in cryptography, writes: "Perhaps the Voynitch manuscript is a bomb that will explode on the day when it is successfully deciphered." This manuscript is in the possession of Hans P. Kraus of New York, and it is on sale for 160,000 dollars. It is a mediaeval illuminated manuscript of 204 pages, the authorship of which is attributed to the Franciscan scholar, Roger Bacon. According to the pagination, twenty-eight pages are missing. It is either written in an unknown language or more probably, in code. Towards 1580, the Duke of Northumberland, who had plundered a large number of monasteries, gave it to the magician John Dee, who in turn offered it to the Emperor Rudolf II. In the seventeenth century, the manuscript fell into the hands of the Rector of the University of Prague, who commissioned the brilliant Jesuit, Athanasius Kircher, to decipher it. After his death, it came into the possession of his order, still undeciphered. In 1912, the antiquarian Wilfred Voynitch bought it from the Jesuit College of Mondragone Frascati in Italy and sold copies all over the world. People thought they recognized spiral nebulae, unknown planets and the sky around Aldebaran and the Hyades in the illuminations. In 1921, William Newbold, Dean of Pennsylvania University, thought that he had deciphered the beginning of the manuscript. In his opinion, Bacon possessed knowledge surpassing our own. Newbold died in 1926, Voynitch in 1930, his wife in 1960 and the heirs sold the mysterious manuscript to Kraus, who now awaits an offer from some wealthy foundation.

Absolutely any theory is admissible. The pessimist will remember the famous Rhind papyrus, dating to 1800 B.C., which announced "the complete knowledge of everything, the explanation of everything that exists and the revelation of all secrets," and merely contained the theory of fractions and its application to the payment of workmen on a building-site. The optimist will assume that Roger Bacon did not write down such trivia in code. Either the Voynitch manuscript contains only out of date receipts or it is a secret key and will revolutionize the state of our knowledge one day.

This revolution is already under way, mainly through the study of ancient mathematics. Even van de Waerden, one of the authorities in this field, supports the theory of an ancient knowledge that gave birth to the Babylonian, Egyptian and Chinese cultures.

It is obvious that the discovery of higher mathematics would prove the existence of great civilizations that were extinguished like the flame of a candle when it is blown out. Higher mathematics require a special mental make-up. Figures have a relationship to the real world. If any traces of them are preserved in the documents at our disposal, they can only be spotted by mathematicians with archaeological training or by teams whose members specialize in a variety of fields.

One last trail might lead to the Great Language: the collective unconscious of the human race. The strange languages that children sometimes invent, the unknown languages that men sometimes speak under hypnosis— are they echoes of the "language of the birds, mother and oldest of languages," which goes back to the beginning of time?

Thirty years ago I visited the gorge of Padirac. The ferryman who rowed us over the dark water spoke these wonderful words: "This river is so unknown that no one even knows its name." In saying this, he expressed two profound truths that are always in the back of our minds. One is that things only exist for us when they have a name, the second is that there has always been a name that corresponds to each thing, a name that is eternal.

Chesterton wrote that man knows that the soul has subtle nuances more miraculous and more numerous than the colors of a wood in autumn. And he asks if we believe that all these shades of meaning can be accurately expressed by an arbitrary system of grunts and groans. If a stock exchange runner can really bring forth all the sounds needed to express the mysteries and memory of the agonies of desire.

He says that no thinking person believes that any language is adequate for the purpose, that perhaps every language has degenerated since the sacred age when Adam gave things their names.

He asks if this idea is nostalgia or the declaration of eternal inadequacy. And whether the myth of a great language was invented to alleviate the anguish men feel in the face of the inexpressible.

Nevertheless, he continues, tradition persistently refers to it and the gnostic sects claimed to hold the secret of books the origin of which was allogeneous, foreign and superior to this world. Then he quotes these solemn words from the conclusion of the Holy Book of the Great Invisible Spirit:

"This is the book written by the great Seth (one of Adam's sons). He placed it in the lofty mountains.. . . The great Seth wrote this book in the writings of a hundred and thirty years. He placed it in the mountain called Charax, so that it may be shown at the end of time and at the last moments."

# 3 In Search of a Language of the Absolute

How did the Revelation take place? Whenever we dream regretfully of writings that have disappeared, the idea of one great original language expressing the knowledge of the legendary gods constantly recurs.

There was a man who dreamt of conquering the moon three hundred years ago and also wanted to create a new great language. His name was John Wilkins and he was the first secretary of the Royal Society. Wilkins was the friend of Elias Ashmole, who bequeathed to Oxford a museum rich in documents about alchemy and Freemasonry. A member of the Rosicrucians, he was the pupil of the alchemist William Backhouse. In his diary for 13 May, 1653, we read: "My master Backhouse, who is lying ill at his house in Fleet Street and feels that his end is near, revealed the secret of the philosopher's stone to me at eleven o'clock this evening."

Backhouse and his kindred spirits, Elias Ashmole and Wilkins, felt that the time had come to turn the secret science into a public one. The newly-founded Royal Society was to give a new stimulus to research. These men had unusual power of imagination and intellectual curiosity. Jorge Luis Borges, who has devoted a penetrating study to Wilkins, says that his main interests were theology, music, the manufacture of transparent hives for observing bees, the construction of spaceships for a regular service to the moon and the creation of a universal language. As Master of Wadham College, Oxford, Wilkins founded a scholarly society in that city. It was called the "invisible college" and included such eminent scholars

95

as Sir Christopher Wren and Robert Boyle among its members. The college joined up with the Royal Society, which was given its charter in 1662 by King Charles II.

Wilkins was also friendly with the members of a platonic group at Cambridge of which Newton was the guiding spirit from 1670 to 1680. This group re-edited essential alchemical texts in a collection supervised by Ashmole, the *Theatrum Chimicum Britannicum*. Robert Boyle had already published his book *The Sceptical Chemist* (1661), in which he claimed that all theoretical assertions ought to be proved experimentally. He believed that the four basic elements of the Greek philosophers, earth, air, fire and water, were not enough to describe matter, since it was undoubtedly composed of a large number of elements. In effect, we know of 108 elements today. In addition to having a profound knowledge of ancient secrets, the members of the invisible college were passionately interested in experiments and were conscious of opening up to mankind the way to a more complete mastery of nature.

In this atmosphere of enthusiasm and in an environment in which people were convinced that hitherto impossible undertakings could be carried out, Wilkins worked on the construction of a universal language. The Great Language had obviously existed at one time and perhaps it would be rediscovered one day. But Wilkins was unwilling to wait so long. He set about creating a universal language for the men of his time that was intended to describe reality and its laws. He worked on it for four years, from 1664 to 1668. The result was a book of 600 pages, entitled *An Essay toward a Real Character and a Philosophical Language* and published in 1668. Today it is completely forgotten.

It was Wilkins' ambition to create a language in which each word, by defining itself, transmitted a complete knowledge of the thing represented and situated it in the categories of reality. He began by dividing the universe into forty categories or genera, which could in turn be subdivided into species. He allotted a monosyllable with two letters to each category, a consonant to each sub-category and a vowel to each species.

Thus, *de* means an element, *deb* the first of the elements, fire, and *deba* a flame.

In the nineteenth century, that hot-bed of Utopian philosophy and literature, when Charles Fourier's *Le Nouveau Monde amoureux* (1829) and the socialist novel *Voyage en Icarie* by Etienne Cabet appeared, a linguist called Letellier remembered Wilkins and adopted his method. He now proposed a language in which *a* meant animal, *ab* mammifer, *abo* carnivore, *aboj* feline, *aboje* cat, *abi* herbivore, *abiv* one of the equidae, etc. The Spaniard Bonifacio Sotos Ochando tried the same kind of system around 1850.

"The words in Wilkins' analytical language," writes Borges, "are not crude arbitrary symbols. Each of the letters which compose it is significant, as the letters of the Holy Scriptures were to the Cabbalists." Children could understand this language without knowing that it was artificial. Later they would gradually discover that it was not only a language, but also a key to the world. The word "salmon," for example, does not tell us anything. In Wilkins's language, *zana* tells us that it is a river fish with scales and reddish flesh. "Theoretically," continues Borges, "it is not impossible to conceive of a language in which the name of each being would indicate all the details of its past and future destiny." Léon Bloy wrote in *L'Ame de Napoléon* (1926): "There is not a single human being who can say who he is . . . No one knows what he has come to do in this world, what his actions, feelings and thoughts relate to, nor what is his true name, his imperishable name in the register of light."

Every thing and every being is, without our knowing its importance in the overall composition, like a full stop, a comma, or a verse or a whole chapter of a great liturgical text, whose alphabet, vocabulary and grammar are hidden from us. We are the verses, the words or letters in this magic book, and this never-ending book is the only thing which exists in the world. It is the world.

This was the great idea that obsessed Wilkins when he tried to develop a language that transmitted detailed knowledge about each and every thing, according to its role in our inadequate knowledge of the universe. This kind of enterprise naturally comes up against the difficulty of dividing up all the elements of our universe into classes. In other words, it depends on the conception we have of the world at a particular time, and the classification can only be arbitrary and speculative. An ancient Chinese encyclopaedia, *The Heavenly Market of Benevolent Knowledge,* for example, divides up animals as follows: belonging to the Emperor, lamed, embalmed, behaving like mad things, drawn with a fine camel-hair brush, looking like flies from a distance, etc.

As a scientist of his time, Wilkins naturally proposed a scheme of classification that seems unsatisfactory to us today. Thus he subdivided stones, his eighth category, into ordinary stones (flint, gravel, slate), comparatively dear ones (marble, amber, coral), precious stones (pearls, opals), transparent ones (amethysts, sapphires) and insoluble ones (coal, clay, arsenic). We have made advances in nomenclature and classification since then. But we have also learnt that the more our knowledge of reality increases, the more ambiguities occur. For example, should we classify light in the category "waves" or in the category "particles"? It would be a good idea if a Wilkins of our own time tried and fed his universal language into a computer which, after examining all the possible combinations, could produce the missing words. They would probably stand for non-existent or impossible objects, for example, a four-sided triangle, gaps in the universe or the stable element with a nucleus consisting of five particles. One might also ask whether the rules of such a synthetic language would not correspond to some fundamental mystery of words and numbers.

But let us return to Wilkins. He stood on the threshold

between tradition and modern science. In a letter dated November, 1629, Descartes had already mentioned that with the help of the decimal system of numeration, we could learn to name all the quantities up to infinity in a single day and to write them down in a new language— the language of figures. He suggested the formation of an analogous general language which could embrace and organize all human thoughts. Thirty years later, Wilkins did in fact work on such a project.

The intellectual spirit that animated the "invisible college," which was stimulated both by alchemy and modern ideas, directed its researches to establishing a new language created by and for scholars, since Latin had proved inadequate. The universalist ideas of the Renaissance, enriched by Rosicrucian influence and the rise of scientific thought, led to a dream of an "International Group of Men of Knowledge and Ability." And a synthetic language was needed for the creation of such an international group. Today, three hundred years later, this international group is still trying to establish itself.

Lastly, Wilkins' undertaking was based on the religious conception of language. God spoke directly to men. He communicated his orders and prohibitions to them orally. The idea of a Sacred Book, a Holy Scripture, was a subsequent addition.

This is a tenacious and long-lived idea which has been transferred from the mystical to the profane plane. It led the poet Mallarmé to say that everything in the world existed to terminate in a book. The same idea led Flaubert to passion and martyrdom, launched Joyce on the adventure of *Ulysses,* and today makes writers experiment incessantly with the theme that "the written word leads back only to itself."

In Moslem tradition, the Koran, *Al Kitab* or the Book, is one of God's attributes. The original text, or mother of the book, is preserved in heaven. "The Koran is copied in a book, it is spoken with the tongue, it is kept in men's hearts, but its true existence is in God." It is not a work of the Godhead; it partakes of his substance. To the Jewish cabbalists, the magic power of God's command, "Let there be light," emanates from the actual letters of which these words are composed. The God of Israel created the universe with the numbers from one to ten and the twenty-two letters of the alphabet. "Twenty-two basic letters. God drew them, imprinted them, combined them, permutated them and produced with them everything that is and everything that will be."

To the Christians, God has written two books, the Bible and the Universe. In Francis Bacon's view, the Holy Scriptures reveal his will, and the universe, i.e. the book of Nature, reveals his power. The Creation is a book that we have to decipher like the Holy Scriptures. "We cannot understand it," wrote Galileo, "until we have learnt its language and its characters. The language of this book is mathematics and its characters are triangles, circles and other figures."

So the idea is firmly lodged in the human mind that there is an ultimate key to language and an ultimate key-language; that the Word was given to man to solve the puzzle of his own existence and the world; that the "master word" of the absolute structure could emerge from modulations of the human breath; lastly, that our language is only a distorted echo of a vanished or future Great Language.

Wilkins dreamed of a language which would contain the totality of the real. But perhaps there ought to be a language that deals with essentials, rather than everything? In other words, if we wish to communicate with an intelligence in the universe, whatever its nature, then there must be a language through which terrestrial intelligence can make itself understood and receive answers. A Great Language as a means of communication with the infinite? Wilkins, who had no doubt that men would land on the moon one day, wanted to equip them with a language in which they could describe their own world.

Their vocabulary was to be a universal encyclopaedia. Today we are trying to create a language with which we can send the following simple message into outer space: "There is Being here! We think! Answer!" In other words, we are asking ourselves what language we should use so that we can be included in the telephone directory of the Milky Way. We are seeking for a Holy Grail of language, for a language of the absolute.

By means of rocket *sondes*, we receive signals from heavenly bodies millions of light-years away from the earth. Perhaps we shall find one day that there is an interspatial telegraph system. Some authors have proposed astonishing solutions as possible answers to the problem of this language. There are, for example, the "Speedtalk" invented by the writer Robert Heinlein, "Loglan," short for logical language, proposed by a group of American semanticists, and lastly "Lincos," *lingua cosmica,* which the Dutch logician Hans Freudenthal is trying to construct.

In all three cases, they are entirely artificial languages, logical compendia capable of expressing the essence of intelligence.

Heinlein's first observation is that all the languages available to us at present are inadequate. The mind loses a large part of its substance when it comes into contact with words. Every expression is only minimally a message from the intelligence; it is far more what results from its struggle against barriers. So Heinlein conceived a music-vocabulary. It is limited, but subtle, flexible and easy to use. Accents and vowels multiply the relatively small number of sounds that the human throat can produce. Such a language would enable us to think quicker by expressing ourselves quicker and also to experience more, i.e. to increase the time when we are genuinely conscious. By 400 to 800 per cent, Heinlein claims. This language can easily be registered by electronic machines printing the symbols from dictation speeded up four to eight hundred times. Lastly, Heinlein assures us, Speed-talk is a language without paradoxes, for paradoxes arise from the conflict between the infinitely supple, ductile, multi-levelled mind and the linear dualistic structures of our written and spoken modes of expression. It is a language that is adapted to the real structure of the world and the mind, borrowing speed and ductility from mathematics and its countless modulations from music.

We can compare Heinlein's fantasy with the work of Benjamin Lee Whorf, a chemist whose hobby is linguistics. He discovered an Indian tribe whose language was conceived in terms of relativity and quantas rather than in terms of space and time. This language has conjunctions that correspond to an event in space-time. Thus a conjunction has three modes which can be applied to the event man-boat: the mode of the real, when the event, a man in a boat, has actually been observed; the dream mode, used when the speaker has experienced the situation in a dream, and the mode of the probable, when the speaker has not seen something himself, but only heard about it.

The objection has been made to Heinlein's language that it presupposes a perfect ear and perfect instruments of transmission. Unless one has the ear of a Mozart, one might hear "spiceship" when someone says "spaceship." Heinlein, who, incidentally, has so far only dreamed of such a language, answers that the very fact of learning Speedtalk and being able to receive it without error will prove that one already belongs to the species *homo novus* who will succeed *homo sapiens*. However, he devotes himself very seriously to his dream language and his ideas have stimulated scientific circles, such as the group studying Loglan (Logical language). This language, which is less revolutionary than Heinlein's, has not freed itself from Latin and Anglo-Saxon roots, but it is constructed in such a way as to eliminate ambiguity as far as is humanly possible.

\* \* \*

There is something fine and great about these ambitious projects, whether they are leaps into an imaginary future or preliminary studies. They postulate that a new language would create a new man. We hear the echo of the cabbalistic myth. The restoration of the lost language would restore man to his divine condition. This traditional idea also links up with topics that are currently preoccupying scholars.

In his opening lecture as Professor of Molecular Biology at the Collège de France, in 1967, Jacques Monod, the Nobel prize-winner, said: "The appearance of language may have preceded the formation of the central nervous system peculiar to man and may have contributed decisively to the selection of the variants most apt to use all its resources."

From a new language suitable for activating the higher functions of the mind, we pass, with the logician Freudenthal, to a language with which we can reach intelligences in outer space. Freudenthal's first book about Lincos appeared in 1960 in the series *Studies in Logic and the Foundations of Mathematics,* in which teachers of mathematical logic such as Brouwer, Beth and Heyting were already represented. It is entitled *Design of a Language for Cosmic Intercourse.* Freudenthal's Lincos is in fact aimed at extraterrestrial communication and presupposes a universal structure of intelligence, whatever form the beings that house this intelligence in distant stars may take. The Dutch logician tries to establish a system of radio signals capable of describing our life in the three forms of time, space and behavior to the extra-terrestrial intelligence through the cosmic night and the medium of mathematics. Freudenthal writes: "It is probable that my cosmic language already exists and that beings use it to communicate. I had thought that cosmic rays might be the vehicle for such communications, but I no longer think so.—It is possible that the waves used are stopped by the earth's atmosphere or the electrical layers situated above it. It may be that an outpost on space detects these

103

cosmic conversations. But as we know nothing about intelligent galactic beings, what can there be in common between them and us?" In Freudenthal's view, mathematical intelligence and the space-time concept.

The Lincos language depends on the emission of long and short waves, a whole vocabulary of signals, which express the essence of methematics, the passage of time and the nature of space in our region of the heavens. With the help of Lincos, we earth-men are seeking a dialogue with the universe. Part IV of the book is a treatise on space, motion and mass, telling the "others" how we measure distance and velocities, the variations of mass in terms of velocity, the laws of gravity, etc. These messages, circulating in the ocean of light-years, could, in thousands of years' time, inform us that there is intelligent mind there, and indicate our position. "That may be a great day for the "others". Unless they calmly note down in their archives that the ten thousandth civilization in the $n$th galaxy has just been picked up. And continue their researches with a cold indifference, the reason for which we cannot fathom, the universe being perhaps, as Carl Sagan envisages, "full of civilizations which listen, but do not send out any signals." We cannot easily free ourselves from the terror of eternity, the dread of the boundless. Beneath the populous heavens, the mind utters the long plaint of its limitations, like a dog baying the moon. But it may be that someone is also seeking us with love, that each intelligence seeks the others in order to increase its stature through contact with them and discover in them an absolute structure.

Should we do everything in our power to attract attention? Shall we discover the Enemy, or the universality of the divine creature, as Teilhard de Chardin and C. S. Lewis believed, i.e. a supreme vibration and illumination of the spirit, common to every intelligent creature, whether man or "vaporous brains of the spiral nebulae"?

A deficiency of language separates us from our essential nature, as it separates us from the nature of the "others", and we seek the Great Language that will give us back communication with the being of Being, on earth and in the heavens. "No! No; Do not seek that, it is impious and dangerous," cried Arthur Clarke, in a moment of depression. "We do not know what walks the high road between the galaxies and it is better if we do not know."

But we must play with fire. It was by playing with fire that man built his home on earth.

# PART THREE

# The Greatest Question of All

# 1 The Mysterious Akpallus

Many publications containing interesting conclusions drawn from research are only discussed in limited scientific circles, which explains why a sensational book by J. S. Schlovski, Director of the Astronomical Institute of Moscow University, passed almost unnoticed. This is an astounding fact, for its comprehensive information, serious scholarship and daring theories make it one of the most illuminating works dealing with life and intelligence in the universe. Schlovski ignores the doctrines of the experts and academic and political prejudices, and invokes the patronage of poets and visionaries when advancing his reasoning.

Carl Sagan, Professor of Astronomy at Harvard University and Director of the Astrophysical Observatory at Cambridge, Mass., had the Russian book translated. All kinds of ideas occurred to him when he read it. He wrote to Schlovski and proposed a joint edition of the American version. The Russian answered sceptically: "The chances of the two of us collaborating are less than those of a visit to earth by extra-terrestrial beings." But he was mistaken. In 1966, Sagan published the book, with the English version alternating with the text of his Russian colleague and his notes. *Intelligent Life in the Universe* is the first and as yet the only book that had been written by two scholars from east and west about the most remarkable project of our time—making contact with intelligences in the cosmos. The American edition is dedicated to the memory of the biologist J. B. S. Haldane, member of the Academy of Sciences of the USA and the Academy of the Soviet Union, who died in India in 1964, and it begins with an Ode by Pindar:

"There is a race of men, there is a race of gods,
Both draw the breath of life from the same mother,
But the powers are separated,
So that men are nothing
And the others are masters of the luminous heavens
Which are their citadel for ever.
Yet we all share in the great intelligence,
We have some of the strength of the immortals,
Although we do not know what the day has in store for us,
What destiny has prepared for us before the night falls."

Then comes an introduction by Schlovski:

"The idea that beings endowed with reason existed not only on the earth, but also in countless other worlds appeared in the distant past when astronomy was still in its infancy. The Buddhist religion has a vague conception of the number of inhabited worlds. According to its concept of the transmigration of souls, sun, moon and fixed stars are the places to which the souls of the dead make their way before they enter the bliss of Nirvana.

"The progress of astronomy has given the idea of a multiplicity of inhabited worlds a firmer foundation. To the Greek philosophers, the earth was not the only seat of intelligence. We can but bow to their brilliant intuition when we remember what the standard of science was at the period. Thus, in the sixth century B.C. Thales, the natural philosopher, taught that the stars were made of the same matter as the earth. His pupil, Anaximander, declared that worlds would appear and disappear. Anaxagoras, indeed thought that the moon was inhabited and even saw in the 'germs of life,' which were present everywhere, including the cosmos, the origin of all living things. During the centuries that followed and right down to our own period, various philosophers have re-adopted the idea of 'panspermy', according to which life has always existed. The Christian religion was quick to adopt this concept of the 'germs of life.'

"The materialistic school of Epicurus taught that a great number of inhabited worlds, similar to our earth, existed. Mitrodorus believed that to consider the earth as the only inhabited world in boundless space was as stupid as the assertion that only one ear of wheat could grow in a vast field. It is interesting that by 'worlds' the followers of this doctrine did not simply mean planets, but also every kind of heavenly body in the infinite expanses of the cosmos. Lucretius passionately defended the idea that the number of inhabited worlds was incalculable. In his didactic poem *De Rerum Natura,* he says: 'Man must realize that there are other regions in the universe, other earths than our own and different races of men.'

"Then the Christian religion made the earth the center of universe for one and a half thousand years. It was the astronomer Copernicus who first showed men the place that was really their due. Then the hypothesis that there might be life on other planets received a scientific foundation. The first observations of the heavens with a telescope, by which Galileo initiated a new era in astronomy, aroused the imagination of his contemporaries. It was obvious that the planets were heavenly bodies closely resembling the earth. That raised the following question. If there were mountains and valleys on the moon, why not towns with inhabitants endowed with reason, too? Why should our sun be the only star which is surrounded by planets? The great Italian philosopher and astronomer, Giordano Bruno, expressed this daring idea unequivocally: 'There is an immense number of earths that revolve round their suns, as our seven planets revolve round our sun . . . Living beings inhabit these worlds.' The Catholic Church took a terrible revenge on Bruno. He was found guilty of heresy by the Inquisition and burnt at the stake in Rome on 17 February, 1600. This was not the last crime against knowledge committed by the church. It continued to oppose the heliocentric theory bitterly until the end of the seventeenth century. But gradually even the theologians realized that such a battle was in vain and they revised their point of view. Today they no longer see any contradiction with the dogmas of their religion in the possible existence of beings on other planets.

"In the second half of the seventeenth and during the eighteenth century, philosophers and writers constantly discussed the problem of whether there was life in the universe.

"I need only mention Cyrano de Bergerac, Fontenelle, Huygens, Voltaire, Lomonossov, Kant and Laplace. The idea of a vast number of inhabited worlds was widespread and hardly anyone dared to oppose it in scientific and philosophical circles. Only scattered voices queried the possibility of all planets being inhabited by living creatures. In a book published in 1853, the many-sided scholar, William Whewell, wrote that life could not exist on all the planets, because the largest of them consisted of gas, water, and vapors, and those that were nearest the sun were exposed to too great a heat. He also tried to prove that there was no life on the moon. Towards the end of the nineteenth century, the astronomer Charles Pickering stated most persuasively that the alterations in the lunar landscape could be explained by large masses of insects changing their habitat. (In passing, I should point out that this theory has been revived since then and applied to Mars.) The Anglo-German astronomer, Friedrich Wilhelm Herschel, even thought that the sun was inhabited. He interpreted sun spots as rifts in the dazzling clouds which enveloped the dark side of the star. In his opinion, they enabled the inhabitants of the sun to admire the starry vaults.

"At the end of the nineteenth century, the old theory of panspermy cropped up again in a new guise. According to this metaphysical conception, life has existed in the universe for all eternity. The stuff of life did not proceed from lifeless matter according to fixed laws, but was transmitted from planet to planet. Fine dust, driven by the pressure of light, carried living matter, spores or bacteria, to other planets. If they found favorable conditions on a particular planet, the spores germinated and initiated the evolution of life.

"If we cannot summarily dismiss the possibility of such transference of life, it is still hard to imagine such a process. The Swedish Nobel prize-winner, Svante Arrhenius, assumed that light could impart considerable speed to the specks of dust, but what we know about the nature of interstellar space today excludes this possibility. Lastly, the theory of eternal life is irreconcilable with the idea that we have formed of the stars and the galaxies on the basis of extensive observations. According to this concept, the universe in the past consisted solely of hydrogen or hydrogen and helium, while the heavy elements, without which no form of life is conceivable, only appeared later.

"Moreover, on the basis of the shift of the Milky Way's spectrum towards red, we can assume that the state of the universe ten or fifteen million years ago precluded the existence of life.

"In other words, life could only have appeared in certain privileged regions at a specific stage of evolution, and so the cornerstone of the theory of panspermy has turned out to be erroneous.

"The Russian Konstantin Tsiolkovski, the father of astronautics, was a fervent champion of the hypothesis of a large number of inhabited worlds. Here are two quotations from his works: 'Can we imagine Europe being inhabited and the other parts of the world not?' And: 'The individual planets represent different phases of the development of life. If we ask the planets, we can learn what mankind was several thousands of years ago and what it will be in a few million years...' If the first quotation is reminiscent of the classical philosophers, the second one contains a very significant idea which has since been further developed. The thinkers and writers of past centuries conceived of the civilizations of other planets as having similar social orders to our own. Tsiolkovski rightly drew people's attention to the considerable

113

difference in standards between the cultures of different worlds. But at the time his theories could not be confirmed scientifically.

"The idea of a large number of inhabited worlds is closely linked with the theories of the origin of the world. In the first third of the twentieth century a theory was advanced claiming that the sun acquired its planets as the result of an extremely rare cosmic catastrophe (a collision between two stars). This theory was widely upheld and so most scholars considered life as an exceptional phenomenon in the universe. It was thought very unlikely that in our galaxy, which contains more than a hundred million stars, there was a single one with a planetary system, apart from the sun. Today we assume that there are many planetary systems in our galaxy and that the solar system is the rule, rather than the exception. Nevertheless, this hypothesis, although extremely probable, is still not proven.

"The advances of stellar cosmogony have contributed decisively to the solution of the problem of the appearance and evolution of life in the universe. We now know which stars are young and which are old, and for how long they radiate energy that is constant enough to maintain life on the planets revolving around them. Lastly, with the help of stellar cosmogony, the future of the sun can be predicted over a long period and this is naturally of vital importance for the future of life on earth, too.

"The problem of life is mainly a chemical one. How and owing to what external circumstances did the synthesis of complex organic molecules take place that resulted in the appearance of the first bits of living matter? In the past few decades, biochemists have made considerable progress with this problem, basing themselves mainly on laboratory experiments. However, I believe that delving deeply into the problem of the origin of life on earth and other planets has only become possible very recently. We have just begun to raise a corner of the veil that hides the holy of holies of the living substance: heredity.

"The extraordinary successes of genetics and especially the deciphering of the 'cybernetic meaning' of desoxide ribonucleic acid and ribonucleic acid call the definitions of life itself in question. It becomes more and more obvious that the problem of the origin of life is a genetic problem. With the help of the recently developed science of microbiology, its solution is undoubtedly close.

"A new chapter in the history of the idea of a large number of inhabited worlds began on 4 October, 1957, when the earth's first satellite was put into orbit in the Soviet Union. All of a sudden men realized that they inhabited a rather small planet floating in the eternity of cosmic space. Of course, most of us had learnt a little astronomy at school, but practical activity was still guided by the belief that the earth is the center of the universe. So it cannot be over-emphasized what a revolution in men's consciousness took place when this new era of our history began, the era of the conquest of the cosmos.

"For a long time the question of the existence of life in other worlds was posed in abstract terms; now at last it acquired concrete significance. In a few years, it will be answered experimentally. 'Life detectors' will be sent to the surface of the planets to inform us about possible forms of life there. Soon astronauts will land on the moon,[1] Mars and possibly on mysterious Venus. Then life on those stars, if any is discovered, can be investigated with biological methods.

"This book about intelligent life in the universe will inform the layman about the state of research at the time of writing. I emphasize 'at the time of writing', because our ideas about the possibility of large numbers of inhabited worlds are constantly changing. Unlike other books which are mainly concerned with the planets of the solar system, especially Mars and Venus, I have given preference to the 'other' planetary systems."

\* \* \*

[1] Schlovski wrote and published the text quoted here in 1966, i.e. three years before the first landing on the moon.

Then Schlovski follows up the dreams of the provincial schoolmaster, Konstantin Tsiolkovski. At the beginning of our century, Tsiolkovski foresaw how man would conquer space, utilize the sun's heat and light, settle on the stars and "drive the small planets as we drive horses". He also sketched out the structure of other civilizations in distant galactic systems. "Why should we not conceive the possibility of highly organized beings endowed with reason altering the qualities of whole stellar systems? Perhaps the remarkable phenomena to be observed at the core of the galaxies are attributable to the initiative of unknown civilizations?" And lastly he asks: "Why should we not postulate that the exceptionally strong radio-electric radiation from many galaxies is a formative process of highly organized matter?" Simultaneously he envisages counter-arguments that would inevitably lead "to the melancholy realization of our solitude in the universe", but he rejects them. "We hope", he says, "that the 'cosmic miracles' we observe are miracles of the intelligences in other worlds, evidence of the existence of 'the masters of the luminous heavens which are their citadel for ever'."

This fantastic fairylike prospect raises a question. Was our planet visited in the past by astronauts who came from other planetary systems? As is well known, this is a theory that is being seriously discussed.

When we wrote about the Soviet scholar Agrest's studies of this subject in *Le Matin des magiciens* in 1960 and in our review *Planète* in 1961, the French intellectuals laughed us to scorn. We remember that Louis Aragon himself attacked us because he claimed that Agrest was a harmless buffoon and that in its infinite goodness the Soviet Writers' Union tolerated his idle ravings. Agrest's studies date from 1959. Eight years later Carl Sagan and Schlovski jointly declared: "Agrest's way of tackling the problem seems very reasonable and deserves detailed analysis."

Agrest's chain of thought is essentially as follows: Firstly he assumes that astronauts have visited our globe and

116

encountered men. Such an unusual event would inevitably have left its traces in legends and myths. To primitive peoples these beings would have been gods endowed with supernatural powers. Undoubtedly the heavenly visitors would have been able to transmit technical skills and higher knowledge to the awestruck but curious earth-dwellers.

It is well known that myths and legends depending on an oral tradition have great historical value. At present, the pre-colonial history of the peoples of black Africa is being studied with the help of their myths and stories. Carl Sagan adds this example. In 1786, the Indians of North-West America watched La Pérouse land. A century later, it was possible to reconstruct the French navigator's arrival down to a detailed description of his two ships by analyzing the legends inspired by the event.

If we imagined that La Pérouse and his crew were visitors from another planet, we should have quite a serviceable criterion for the amount of truth in cosmic myths, but we should also have proof of how simple it is to mythify purely terrestrial events and build up a fraudulent career based on similar manipulations of tradition and history. We do not automatically think that everything questionable is a swindle, for we do not think we have a monopoly of the truth. We do not look on science as a sacred cow and we would rather be dead than have the job of censoring the imagination of certain "research workers". Lastly, we know, although unfortunately it is not generally known, that a lot of people cannot do without swindles. But since the publication of *Le Matin des magiciens*, the public has been literally flooded with books that speculate about the same subject. We just want to warn our readers that we take no responsibility for our dubious epigoni.

"As far as we know", Schlovski declares, "there is not a single material monument from past cultures that really entitles us to see in it a reference to thinking beings who came from the cosmos." That is our opinion, too.

117

It is quite possible, for example, that the celebrated fresco at Tassili, in the Sahara, which depicts a "Martian" in a space-suit, has been improperly adduced as proof. (We ourselves are not innocent in this respect, but others have really overdone it.) However, we believe, like Sagan and his Russian colleague, "that research in this direction is neither absurd nor unscientific. But we must keep our heads."

Shall we have visits from outer space? Have beings from the universe already been on earth? In Sagan's estimation the number of technically developed civilizations existing simultaneously in the Milky Way could be of the order of $10^6$. The duration of the existence of such civilizations would be about $10^7$ years. Schlovski remarks: "This seems optimistic to me." Sagan assumes that these civilizations study the cosmos according to a plan which excludes the repetition of a visit. If each civilization sends out a research spaceship every terrestrial year, the average interval between two visits from one and the same star would equal $10^5$ years. In the framework of Sagan's hypotheses, we can reckon about five millennia as the average interval between two visits from one and the same planetary system (our own, for example) sheltering forms of life endowed with reason. If our history really begins with Sumer and if a visit from the cosmos gave this culture its start, we ought to expect a new landing soon. If, as Sagan writes, "it seems probable the earth has received visits from galactic civilizations on many occasions, and probably $10^4$ during the geological era", why do we not find any tangible trace of them?

There are three answers to this question.

Firstly, scientific archaeology is still in its infancy; it undoubtedly still has surprises in store for us and the idea of a cosmo-history may open up new directions for research.

Secondly, we do find traces in men's memories, in legends and myths, but we have not analyzed them deeply

118

enough yet. (Here Sagan names as an example the legend of the Akpallus, or "Fishmen", to which we shall return shortly.)

Thirdly, contacts with beings as primitive as the inhabitants of the earth were in past millennia would not have justified the establishment of a terrestrial base. This base could be on the far side of the moon and perhaps we shall only find the visiting cards of the galactic beings when we have reached an adequate technical standard.

Drake and Clarke have even suggested that an extraterrestrial civilization could have set up an automatic alarm system. For example, its function might be to analyse the content of radioactive elements in the earth's atmosphere. An increase in atmospheric radio isotopes caused by repeated nuclear tests would set off the alarm. As far as our earth is concerned, where radioactivity is growing constantly, this would mean that the warning system somewhere in the cosmos had already sounded the alarm.

Sagan writes: "Forty light-years distant from the earth the news of a new technical civilization takes flight among the stars. If there are beings up there who scan the heavens in the expectation of an advanced technological civilization appearing in our region of space, they will learn of our knowledge, for better or for worse. Perhaps a messenger will come to us in a few centuries' time. I hope that we have progressed further, that we have not destroyed everything here, when the visitors arrive from their distant star."

Schlovski, who is more sceptical or less lyrical, at least admits that there is a possibility differing from zero that the earth has had visitors from outer space. And he adds: "Like Agrest, Sagan turns his attention to legends and myths. He singles out the Sumerian epic which relates that strange beings who brought men knowledge appeared at regular intervals in the waters of the Persian Gulf. It is possible that these events took place not far from the Sumerian town of Eridu in the first half of the fourth

119

millennium B.C. Sagan points out that the Sumerian culture suddenly changes from a condition of stagnant barbarianism to a brilliant flowering. Virtually nothing is known about the origin of the Sumerian culture. René Alleau, the historian of alchemy, puts forward an astonishing theory. The Sumerians did not come from the earth, but from the sea. They had lived for a long time on the ocean in villages formed of groups of rafts, and it was not until after an encounter with superior beings who came from outer space that they landed on terra firma and built their cities and developed an advanced culture.

"In my opinion", says Schlovski, "the theories of Agrest and Sagan do not contradict each other. Agrest suggests an interpretation of biblical texts, but these texts go back to Babylonian history. The Babylonians, the Assyrians and the Persians succeeded the Sumerian and Akkadian cultures. So we cannot exclude the possibility that these biblical texts and the myths going back to the pre-Babylonian era are an echo of the same events. Even if this cannot be proved scientifically, hypotheses of this kind are well worth our attention."

Sagan's hypothesis is as follows. Extraterrestrial visitors in diving-suits on board a spaceship based in the sea transmitted the rudiments of knowledge to men. These men founded Sumer. Mankind must have preserved the memory of these fishmen for a long time (the armor that looked like shining scales, the tail-like breathing apparatus forming an extension of the body), who came from an unknown world to pass on their knowledge. The sign of the fish, which subsequently became the emblem of the initiates in the Near East, may have been connected with these legendary memories.

There are three texts dating from classical times that refer to the Akpallus, but they are all based on Berosos, who was High Priest of Bel-Marduk at Babylon in the days of Alexander the Great. Berosos is reputed to have had access to cuneiform and hieroglyphic accounts that were several thousand years old. Sagan refers mainly to the Greek and Latin accounts collected in Cory's *Ancient Fragments*, quoting the revised edition of 1870. It contains three tales.

## The Account of Alexander Polyhistor

In the first book about the history of Babylon, Berosos mentions writings preserved in Babylon and covering a cycle of fifteen myriads of years. These writings tell the history of the heaven and the ocean, the birth of mankind, as well as the history of the omnipotent beings. Berosos writes that Babylon extended from the Tigris to the Euphrates and that it was a land where wheat and barley flourished. here were also palm-trees, apple trees and most of the fruits, fishes and birds known to us. The part of the country bordering on Arabia was barren, but the other part was fertile and full of valleys. At that time Babylon attracted the peoples of Chaldaea, who lived like beasts of the field.

Then an animal endowed with reason called Oannes appeared. He came from the Persian Gulf. The body of the animal was like a fish. He had a second head underneath his fish's head. He had human feet, but his body finished in a fish's tail. During the day, this creature spoke to men, but did not eat. It instructed them in the arts and sciences, and taught them how to write. It taught them how to build houses, erect temples, practice law and use the principles of geometry. It also taught them to harvest wheat and fruit. At sunset the creature dived into the sea again, for it was amphibious.

## The Account of Abydenus

It is said that Alorus was the first king of Chaldaea. He claimed that God had ordained him to be the people's shepherd. After him, Alaparos reigned, then Amillaros from Pantibiblon. During his reign, a creature like Oannes, called Annedotus, emerged from the sea. Then came the reign of Magalaros, also from Pantibiblon. At this time, four two-headed creatures came out of the sea. They were called Euedocus, Eneugamus, Eneuboulos and Anementus.

## The Account of Apollodorus

Here, writes Apollodorus, is the story as Berosos transmitted it to us. He says that the king of the Chaldaeans was Alorus of Babylon. Then came Alaparus and Amelon, who came from Pantibiblon. Then Ammenon from Chaldaea, in whose reign the Annedotos Musaros Oannes emerged from the Persian Gulf. (Alexander Polyhistor puts the event further back in time.) Then came Megalaros from Pantibiblon, followed by the shepherd Daonos, also from Pantibiblon. In his time, an Annedotos again emerged from the Persian Gulf; he, too, looked like his predecessors, half man, half fish. During the reign of Euedoreschus, another being, called Odacon, appeared. Like the others, he came from the Persian Gulf and had the same complicated form, half man, half fish. (All of them, said Apollodorus, have described in detail, according to the circumstances, what Oannes taught them. Abydenus does not mention these apparitions.) Then Amempsinos of Laranchae reigned; he was followed by Otiartes, a Chaldaean, who also came from Laranchae. After the death of Otiartes, his son Xisuthros reigned. It was in that time that the great Flood came.

## Continuation of Alexander Polyhistor's Account

The god Chronos appeared to Xisuthros in a dream and told him that a Flood would take place on the fifteenth day of the month of Daesia and that mankind would be wiped out. So he ordered him to write a history of the origins, progress and last end of all things down to the present, to bury these notes at Sippara, in the city of the Sun, to build a ship and take with him his friends and his nearest relatives. He was to take on board everything that was necessary to maintain life, to collect every species of animal that flies or runs on the earth and to entrust himself to the deep waters. . . . When he asked the god whither he was to proceed, Chronos answered: "To the place where the gods are."

In these fragments, the extraterrestrial origin of the Sumerian culture is clearly stated. A series of strange creatures appears in the course of several generations. Oannes and the other Akpallus appear as "animals endowed with reason", or rather as intelligent beings in humanoid form, wearing helmets and armor, with a "double body". Perhaps they were visitors from a planet that was entirely covered by the oceans (after a biblical-style Flood?). An Assyrian cylinder seal depicts an Akpallu carrying apparatuses on his back and accompanied by a dolphin.

Alexander Polyhistor describes a sudden flowering of the Sumerian culture after the visit of Oannes, which tallies with the conclusions drawn from Sumerian archaeological studies. The Sumerologist, Thorkild Jacobsen, of Harvard University, writes: "Suddenly the picture changes. From its previous obscurity, the Mesopotamian civilization takes concrete shape." Admittedly, since Jacobsen's studies, traces of still older cities have been found in Mesopotamia indicating that development may have been slower. However, the mystery of the visitors remains, backed up by the examination of Assyrian cylinder seals on which Sagan thinks he can make out the sun surrounded by nine planets, with two smaller planets on one side, as well as other representations of systems showing a varying number of planets for each star. The idea of planets surrounding the sun and the stars did not appear until Copernicus, although there were some early speculations of this kind by Greek philosophers.

The remarkable accumulation of inexplicable events described in Near Eastern legends poses a problem. Archaeology has revealed traces of technology, for example, the blast furnace at Ezeon Geber and the glass block weighing three tons buried near Haifa. The appearance of techniques, new ideas and religions in this part of the world, as if it were the crucible of human history, raises this question. Were these regions selected by teachers who came from the stars? If so, how and when did they come? Sagan envisages five possible starting points of visitors from other stars: Alpha Centauri, Epsilon Eridanus, 61 Cygni, Epsilon Indi and Tau Ceti, fifteen light-years away from us. And he continues: "Stories like the legend of Oannes and the oldest pictures and texts referring to the appearance of the first terrestrial civilizations (until now interpreted exclusively as myths or aberrations of the primitive imagination) deserve more detailed critical studies than have hitherto been devoted to them. And these studies should include research relative to direct contacts with an extraterrestrial culture."

We have undoubtedly reached a stage of wealth and power that enables us to investigate our past more exhaustively. It almost seems as if Plato was addressing us, when he writes in his dialogue *Critias:* "Undoubtedly the names of these autochthones have been saved from oblivion, whereas the memory of their work has grown dark, partly because those who had had the oral tradition handed down to them disappeared, partly because so much time had elapsed. In fact, the members of the human race who remained after the disasters and floods survived in a barbarian condition and knew only the names of the princes who had reigned in the land, but very little about their work. So they liked to give these names to their children, although they did not know about the merits of these men in the past and the laws they had introduced, apart from some obscure traditions relative to each of them. Deprived as they and their children were of the necessities of existence for several generations, they turned their minds only to what they had lost and that was their only topic of conversation. What had happened before, in the remote past, was a matter of indifference to them. The study of ancient legends, research into antiquity, those are two things which entered cities simultaneously with leisure on the day when the necessities of existence were guaranteed for some of the citizens, but not before."

These two things which "entered" our cities may give us insights into the connection between time past and time to come; perhaps they will teach us that our immense effort to conquer space is a very ancient and heroic longing for contacts. Perhaps we shall see our origin and our end as two moments of a relation to life and intelligence in the universe. Of course, when we ask ourselves such questions, when we search for primordial traces of a contact and when we question the possibilities of the future, we must bear in mind the Chinese proverb: "He who awaits a horseman should take care not to confuse the noise of the hooves with the beating of his own heart." But we should also remember that it is hope that makes the heart beat faster.

PART FOUR

About the Right to Ask Questions

Do the facial features of this angel from Reims Cathedral, from the second century A.D., already show the promise of a rising civilization?

Les penseurs (the thinkers)

Who's Who?

There is no explanation for his isolation, nor for the stagnation in his technological and cultural development.

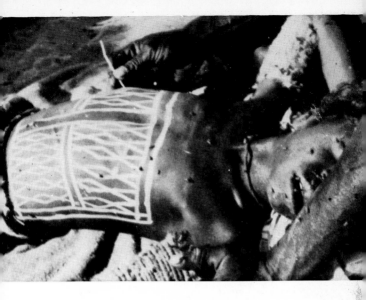

They came in order to show themselves to the white men and to each other.

The king worships in service of the godhead with the lion shoulders. This is narrated by an inscription in Yazilikaya, in the Hurrite language.

The most famous masterpiece from the middle kingdom: The procession of Yazilikaya, cut out in the rocks.

Two sphynxes are still standing guard on the ruins of the capital of the Hethites, now the Turkish village of Aladja Höyük.

The Hethites were true masters of expressive art in the East.

Facial expression and dagger are reminiscent of another mysterious people, that of Luristan in Western Persia.

Sa-oud, king of Uruk, grandson of Lugalkisalsi. *(below: left)*

*(Louvre, Paris)*

About 1500 B.C. the worshipper illustrated here lived in Mesopotamia. *(below: right)*

*(Louvre, Paris)*

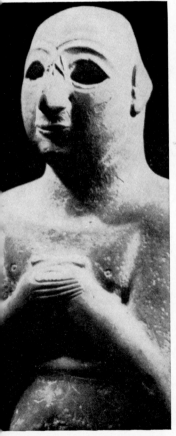

Perhaps the moment is near for us to discover that systematic signals are being sent through space and that somewhere in the Great Ring of Intelligence in the universe telegraphists are busy sending out interstellar telegrams . . .

*Hieroglyphs/Easter Island (Ethnographic Museum, Paris)*

# 1 Pocket Guide for Lovers of Historical Puzzles

"Sir, you believe in profound and wonderful secrets because you are an amateur. There are no secrets for the serious archaeologist."

This was said on television one evening in 1969 by the President of the Association des écrivains scientifiques français (Association of French Scientific Writers). Although he himself was not an archaeologist, but a mathematician, he was defending a position that has become traditional since the Age of Enlightenment. Today, man, who is descended from monkeys and has only been an animal endowed with reason since the death of Louis XVI, has an answer for everything or nearly everything. In his opinion, the best hypothesis is the one which needs the least imagination and does least damage to his preconceived ideas of the world and its workings. If lemmings flock to drown themselves in the ocean, it is because they are shortsighted and think that the sea is a river they can cross. This explanation is "scientific", because it neatly gets rid of an unsolved mystery. It is well known that an essential function of science consists in proving that there is no God. If anyone enthuses over the idea that there is still much that is miraculous and unknown to be illuminated, it is at once assumed that he is on the side of the obscurantists. Yet this "rational science" seems to be motivated more by anti-religious fervor than by reason.

If there are no more mysteries left for the serious archaeologist, why does he bother about archaeology? What a dreary profession! Boucher de Perthes was an amateur. He discovered prehistory. Schliemann was an amateur and he discovered Troy. Hapgood was an amateur. He confirmed the theory of continental drift originated by Wegener, which had been so firmly rejected, although the latter was a scholar. Hawkins was an amateur and he solved the secret of Stonehenge. Nature, which clearly seems to lack an ideology, has forgotten to join the rationalist club. Everything points to the fact that nature is writing a very complicated, imaginative history aimed at people who are open-minded and intelligent rather than academic.

So, Mr. President, the whole of mankind's past will soon be fully charted, will it? In other words, after a few more years of excavations, archaeology will be a complete and compartmented science, like physics in the nineteenth century! There will be no possibility of a revolution in this field comparable to that caused in physics by radio-activity and the theory of relativity.

Allow us to ask a few questions. Who is asking them? Rank amateurs, alas. What, not specialists? No, not specialists in any particular field, but specialists in general ideas. This is a specialty so despised today that we would hardly dare ask questions if we did not remember that the man who asks a lot of questions may sound stupid, but that the man who never asks any will remain stupid all his life.

First kind of question.

No one knows what caused the ice-ages nor how man survived them. We are told *a priori* that there cannot have been any civilizations before the ice-ages—the dates of which, incidentally, are still controversial. As for obvious reasons, we cannot make any excavations in the regions of the earth that are covered with ice in our own day— the Arctic and Antarctic—we should at least leave the question open.

We are told about men living some 15,000 years ago, who were just about able to work stone and keep fire going. These food collectors and hunters knew nothing of agriculture or stock raising. The successive glaciations of the third Riss phase are supposed to have lasted for several thousand years, from 13,000 to about 8,000. What happened to the game and the wild berries then?

Some peoples obviously managed to reach warmer climates; others may have been living there already. But how did those peoples survive when the ice-ages had reached their zenith and the cold had penetrated as far as Central Europe, and all the regions of the world inhabited by the various races of the Palaeolithic were under ice (the only regions, in fact, where we have found traces of them so far).

We think of "stocks", or more specifically stocks of wild wheat, because species of wild wheat existed long before agriculture and also because wheat preserves its qualities, including its nutritive properties, for thousands of years. This has been proved by the discovery in Egyptian tombs of wheat that can still be used.

But even this idea is not so simple. It presupposes the concepts of foresight and planning. To accumulate adequate stocks, prehistoric man must have begun to make them centuries before the advance of the ice-sheet. In other words, he must have predicted what was coming. Have we perhaps seen images of these seers, without realizing it?

This line of reasoning is confirmed by an article which appeared in the Russian review *Technique and Youth* (No. 6, 1965). Here are the facts. In November, 1967, an excavator working on the reconstruction of Hamburg under the direction of the engineer, Hans Elieschlager, dug up some giant stones resembling human heads. Professor Walters Matthes, a German archaeologist, examined them. He succeeded in establishing that they were sculptures made by human hands and dating to the pre-glacial period. In the professor's opinion, they could not be a chance phenomenon. He even found some figures with two faces. When they were turned through one hundred and twenty-five degrees, a man's face turned into a woman's face.

The Russian archaeologist, Z. A. Abramov, has found similar stones. The author of the Russian article, W. Kristly, adds: "The classical cliché of shaggy-haired figures with simian faces, wearing skins and stupidly rubbing two flints together, is a nightmare of classical archaeology which bears no relation to reality." What happened before the ice-ages? One day, the archaeologists and prehistorians will have to admit, for better or worse, that fundamentally they know nothing at all about the subject."

This leads to a second kind of question.

Since 1952, when Daniel Ruzo first began to investigate the plateau of Marcahuasi, which lies at a height of some 12,000 ft. in the heart of the Peruvian Andes, he has continued to find evidence proving the existence in this region of a monumental culture, which could well have been the first and most important in the world.

This discovery was not made by accident. Since 1925, Daniel Ruzo had come to the conclusion that there must be traces of a very ancient civilization in Central and Southern America, especially between the two tropics. He had become convinced of this by studying the Bible, the traditions and legends of mankind, and the analysis of the accounts of the conquest given by the Spanish chroniclers. In 1952, when he heard about an extra-ordinary rock on the plateau of Marcahuasi, he organized an expedition and found out that it was not a single rock, but a vast complex of monuments and sculptures distributed over an area of more than one square mile. Subsequently, he gave the name "Masma" to this putative race of sculptors. In fact, since time immemorial, this name had been used to designate a valley and a town in Central Peru inhabited by the Huancas before the arrival of the Spaniards.

The first thing that struck Ruzo was the existence of an artificial irrigation system for collecting rainwater and distributing it to the whole of the surrounding country during the six dry months of the year. Of the original twelve artificial lakes, only two are still in service. The barrages of the ten others have been destroyed by the ravages of the weather. Channels carried the water 4,500 ft. lower down to irrigate the vast agricultural lands which extended in terraces between the plateau and the valley. These remains prove the prosperity of an isolated region that must have provided nourishment for a very large population.

In order to defend this vital hydrographic center and the fertile countryside, the whole plateau was converted into a fortress. In one place, two enormous cliffs had been deeply hollowed at their base to make direct ascent impossible. At the rear, the two cliffs were connected by a wall of large stones. One is confronted with an enormous rampart, the strategic lay-out of which testifies to the military experience of its constructors. One comes across the remains of well-protected covered roads and, in many places, even little forts the roofs of which have disappeared. One also finds the large stones that formed the walls and the central column that supported the roofs. There were observation posts for the sentries at all points overlooking the three valleys. At many of these posts, enormous stone "teeth" tower up from the ground. They remind us of the ancient war machines used to hurl blocks of stone at the enemy.

Inside the precinct of the fortifications, Daniel Ruzo gradually discovered a large number of sculptures, monuments and tombs. The four most interesting centers, each of them dominated by a monumental altar, are located at the four cardinal points of the compass.

The altars in the east face the rising sun. Opposite them, there is a piece of ground large enough to contain an army or the whole population of the region; nearby a small hill has been artificially treated so that if seen from a certain angle, it looks like a king or a priest seated on a throne, with hands joined in prayer.

133

To the south, at a height of about 180 ft., sculptured stone figures abound. An altar facing west towers 50 ft. above the level of the plain. Below this altar, a steep slope leads down to the plain. It has a smooth surface, as if it had been cemented.

This slope, like those of the other altars, is crossed by lines which indicate that the facing was applied bit by bit to combat the effects of expansion. This cement, which imitates the texture of the natural rock, also seems to cover up several figures. When the research team removed the first layer of this material, they noticed that immediately underneath it there were round projecting bosses which seemed to have been placed there to prevent the cement facing from slipping while it was setting.

Two sculptures which are some distance apart represent Thoueris, the Egyptian goddess of pregnant women, fecundity and the perpetuation of life. She takes the highly original form of a female hippopotamus, standing on its hind legs, with a sort of round cap on its head. With its prominent muzzle, its enormous stomach and the sign of life in its right hand, this conventional figure cannot have been reproduced at Marcahuasi by chance. After the discovery of several figures resembling Egyptian sculptures, Daniel Ruzo thinks that we can envisage the possibility of very ancient contacts between the two cultures.

On the western edge of the plateau, about 100 yards from the abyss, a group of enormous rocks form an altar facing the setting sun. This spot is called the "Mayoralas," a modern name also applied to the young maidens, who, according to tradition, sing and dance at the ritual festivals which take place during the first week in October. The ancient name for this group of singers was "Taquet," a name also used to designate the mass of rocks. There can be absolutely no doubt that it was an altar used for the singing of religious chants and arranged in the form of an acoustic shell to amplify the sound.

The festival begins near San Pedro de Casta on the road which climbs up to the plateau at a place called

134

Chushua, at the foot of a gigantic stone animal. It resembles the fabulous animal conjured up by the imagination of Asiatic artists and is called Huaca-Mallco. Following an ancient tradition, the first ceremony inaugurating the week of festivals in honor of Huari is held one night early in October, before the rainy season. It is celebrated by men only. The other festivals, in which female dancers and singers participate, take place on the outskirts of and inside the village. Even today, these festivities testify to the astonishing vitality of the religious sentiments of the ancient race, preserved down the ages, in spite of savage persecutions and although the original religious motivation has fallen into oblivion.

To the extreme north of the plateau, two enormous frogs squat on a semi-circular altar facing west. Once a year, at the summer solstice, the priests saw the sun rise exactly over the central figure.

This altar forms part of an almost semi-circular group of monuments, in the midst of which there is a mausoleum in a very damaged condition. With the aid of about a hundred photographs taken at different times of the year, Ruzo has found out that the mausoleum consists of the statue of an old man in a recumbent position, watched over by four women, and of four animal figures, which may represent the four natural elements. If the negative of one of these photographs is projected directly on to the screen, a second figure appears. In the place where the head of the first figure was, one sees the carved face of a young man, with his hair hanging down over his forehead, whose mien is proud and noble. How can we explain this sculptural mystery, which is only revealed by the photograph?

The most important of these monuments, because of its excellent workmanship, is a double rock, which is over 80 ft. high. Each of its two parts seems to represent a human head. In reality, at least fourteen men's heads are sculpted and they represent four different races. The rock's most ancient name is "Peca Gasha" (the head of the corridor). Today it is known locally as "La cabeza de Inca" (the Inca's head). As it bears absolutely no resemblance to an Inca's head, it was probably given that name to show that it came from the "dim mists of time". Reference to the accounts of the conquest by the Spanish chroniclers confirms:

That anthropomorphic stone scultpures existed in different regions of Peru and that the Inca Yupanqui knew about them;

that these sculptures were attributed to bearded white men, belonging to a legendary race;

that the Huancas, who inhabited the whole of the part of Central Peru where Marcahuasi and the Masma were at the time of the Spaniards' arrival, have always been looked on as extremely skillful stonemasons;

that this ancient race of stonemasons left inscriptions behind. At Marcahuasi, there are two rocks, unfortunately damaged by the ravages of time, that seem to have been covered with inscriptions.

There are also rock drawings which are quite different from any known hitherto. By a skillful combination of incisions and reliefs the artist has created images which must be looked at from a special point of view. Sometimes the desired effect is achieved when the sunlight falls on them; at others only when it is twilight. It is difficult to study these images properly. In order to grasp all their potentialities, one has to photograph them at different times of the year. Then one can make out fragmentary reproductions of five- and six-pointed stars, circles, triangles and rectangles.

The strangest inscription is on the neck and below the chin of the main figure on the "Inca's head." Imagine double lines made of small black dots indelibly engraved in the rock. The inscription reproduces the central part of a chessboard, or a square grille similar to those which the Egyptians engraved on the heads of their gods.

The memories of the past have gradually been effaced,

in the same way as the stone drawings. It is said locally that the plateau is haunted. They also say that in olden times the best magicians and medicine-men assembled there and that each of the rocks represented one of them. Several figures can be reproduced photographically, but a far larger number can only be appreciated on the spot, under certain conditions of light and then only by sculptors or people with some artistic training. The sculptures are only complete when seen from a specific angle and from certain clearly defined spots. If one moves away from the latter, they change, disappear or change to other figures, which also have to be viewed from special angles. These "points of view" are nearly always indicated by a comparatively important construction or a stone.

Every kind of sculptural technique was used in the execution of these works: bas-relief, engraving and the play of light and shade. Many of them are only visible at certain hours of the day, all the year round in some cases, only at one of the solstices in others, when an extreme solar angle is required. Others again can only be seen at twilight, when no rays of light fall on them.

Many of them are connected with each other and with the corresponding "points of view", so that straight lines can be drawn that link up three or more important points. If some of these lines were extended, they would indicate approximately the extreme positions of the sun's declination.

As we have mentioned, the figures are anthropomorphic and zoomorphic. The former represent at least four human races, including Negroes. Most of the heads have no headgear, but some of them wear a helmet or a hat.

The zoomorphic figures are extremely varied. There are animals native to the region, e.g. condors and frogs, but also animals such as tortoises and monkeys that could not live at this altitude; species important by the Spaniards (cows and horses); animals that did not exist on that continent, even in prehistoric times, such as elephants, African lions and camels, and numerous dogs or dogs' heads, which were the totem of the Huancas even at the time of the conquest.

In executing the sculptures, the sculptors also made use of the effects of light and shade. This can best be appreciated during the months of June and December, when the sun's rays come from the extreme points of its declination. In addition, they utilized the shadows by carving cavities in the rock so that their edges project exact profiles at a particular time of the year to form or complete a figure.

All this leads us to assume the existence in Peru of a race of sculptors who made Marcahuasi their most important religious center and decorated it lavishly for that reason. We could compare this race of sculptors with the prehistoric artists who decorated the caves of Europe with rock paintings. We do, in fact, find rock paintings executed with the help of red, black, yellow and brown indelible varnishes, like others found in the province of Lima, but they are not so old as the great sculptures.

There is a very close relationship between the sculptures of Marcahuasi and those which embellish Easter Island in large numbers. The sculptors' technique is the same. In particular, they represented the heads without eyes, but carved the eyebrows in such a way as to produce a shadow that simulates the eye in the cavity at a certain time of the year.

These works, of an extremely archaic type, seem to have been conceived by a human mentality halfway between that of the Palaeolithic or Mesolithic—of which the Australian aborigines are the last relic—and the familiar mentality of the great empires, the most outstanding characteristics of which are the working of stone, geometry, arithmetic giving relative values, including zero, and the construction of pyramids.

Marcahuasi was apparently not so much a center of dwelling places as of meeting places of sons of the same clan. The whole group of monuments and sculptures on the three square kilometers of the plateau forms a sanctuary like the alignments at Carnac in Brittany or the caves at Les Eyzies in the Dordogne.

Four thousand black-and-white and color photographs, chemical examinations of the stone and comparison with bas-reliefs found in Egypt and Brazil show that the plateau of Marcahuasi may be the site of the oldest culture in the world, older than the Egyptian and Sumerian cultures. But what happened in South America between this period and the arrival of the Spaniards?

So the third kind of question will deal with the methods of establishing chronologies.

If one talks to archaeologists about South America, they become aggressive and break off the conversation after a few slighting remarks such as "superstition," "prelogical mentalities," etc. Ethnologists are generally more accommodating, for example, the Danish Professor Kaj Birket-Smith, doctor of the Universities of Pennsylvania, Oslo and Basle. His book *The Paths of Culture* was published in 1965 by the University of Wisconsin. In it we find the following sentence about South American cultures: "We seem to be faced with an insoluble enigma and we must admit that the final answer has not yet been found."

Whether we assume that South America was colonized from Polynesia, from some mysterious Atlantis or even from Crete (the last-named theory is defended in Honoré Champion's book *Le Dieu Blanc précolombien*), or whether we start from the theory of an indigenous culture, the enigmas multiply and the contradictions accumulate. Let us take the ruined city of Tiahuanaco on Lake Titicava in Bolivia and compare two chronologies of the city: the classical archaeologists' chronology and the romantic archaeologists' chronology.

*The classical chronology:*
9000 B.C.: men closely resembling present-day Indians hunted animals that do not exist today in South America.
3000 B.C.: these men discovered agriculture.

139

1200 B.C.: technology began, especially with the invention of pottery.

800 B.C.: maize became the main source of food.

Between 700 B.C. and A.D. 100: the appearance of vast civilizations and the construction of the cyclopean city of Tiahuanaco.

A.D. 100 to 1000: three civilizations appeared and disappeared.

A.D. 1000 to 1200: no finds and no traditions. The oldest culture during this period, which cannot be dated, is that of Chanapata. Alfred Métraux, a prominent archaeologist, writes of this culture: "One thing is certain. There is a break between this archaic culture and the Inca culture, the beginnings of which date to about 1200 B.C. So far there is no way of filling the gap."

A.D. 1200 to 1400: a series of Inca emperors, whose very existence is doubtful. For safety's sake, serious archaeologists call them semi-legendary.

A.D. 1492: discovery of America.

1532: destruction of the Inca Empire by the Spanish invasion.

1583: the Council of Lima decreed the burning of the knotted cords, or quipus, on which the Incas had recorded their history and that of the civilizations which had preceded them, because they were instruments of the devil. Thus vanished the last chance of learning the truth about the past of Peru. All we can do today, whether we are classicists or romanticists, is to put forward theories.

Here is the *romantic chronology:*

50,000 B.C.: The Masma culture, the oldest in the world, was born on the plateau of Marcahuasi.

30,000 B.C.: foundation of the megalithic empire of Tiahuanaco.

20,000 B.C.: collapse of the empire of Tiahuanaco and birth of the Paititi empire. Development of astronomy.

10,000 B.C. to A.D. 100: five great empires separated by successive catastrophes.

A.D. 1200: Manco Capac founded the Inca empire. After this the romantic chronology rejoins the classical one.

To the layman, the arguments on which the two chronologies are based seem equally valid. Can we settle the debate by resorting to one of the physical methods of dating—radio carbon, thermoluminescence, argon-potassium relation, etc.? Unfortunately all these methods are debatable in principle and delicate to operate, especially carbon 14.

The principle of dating objects by the radio carbon method is simple. The terrestrial atmosphere is constantly bombarded by cosmic rays which come from space. Under the influence of this bombardment, part of the nitrogen in the atmosphere turns into carbon. But this carbon is a heavy, radio-active carbon with the atomic weight 14. Combined with oxygen, it forms radio-active carbon dioxide, which is absorbed by plants. The plants in their turn are eaten by animals and ultimately every living organism contains a certain proportion of carbon 14. When the organism dies, exchanges with the outside world stop. The carbon 14 in the dead organism decreases steadily by periods of 5,600 years. This means that after 5,600 years only half the original carbon is present. After another 5,600 years, only half this half remains, in other words a quarter of the original amount. Using precision instruments, we can count the remaining atoms and so establish when an animal was killed, a tree felled to make charcoal or a mummy placed in its sarcophagus.

That is the principle. It presupposes that cosmic radiation was the same at all times and in all countries, that the sample tested has not been contaminated by recent microbes or bacteria, and that there has not been any exchange with the outside world. In practice, these conditions are never fulfilled. Especially in Peru, phenomena which we are not too clear about and which may be due to the altitude or local radio-activity falsify radio carbon dating, so that the archaeologist, J. Alden Mason, could write in his book *Ancient Peru* (1965): "In general, if a date obtained by radio carbon seems completely unreasonable to the expert archaeologist and if it does not fit in with adjacent dates, he is entitled to reject it and insist on it being checked by other methods." This means that we cannot rely on the radio carbon method for the definitive solution of the Peruvian mystery and that it is legitimate for us to accept the romantic chronology when it is based on experiments. As regards the plateau of Marcahuasi, Daniel Ruzo has carried out some aging experiments with bits of virgin granite, which he exposed to the climate of the plateau. In this way he arrived at a date of the order of 50,000 years. In addition, it would be advisable for the discoloration of the granite to be observed, not with the naked eye, but with the help of photo-electric cells.

Generally speaking, the tendency today is to accept the carbon 14 method as confirmation of an already established date, but not to rely on it too much if there is no additional check. For the moment, the same holds good of other physical methods.

Lastly, the fourth kind of question deals with the mysterious finds and remains of an advanced technology.

H. P. Lovecraft, the father of science-fiction, wrote: "The theosophers and generally speaking everyone who bases their philosophy on Indian tradition speak of enormous periods of past time in terms which would make one's blood run cold, if the whole thing were not proclaimed with saccharine optimism. But what do we really know?"

One of the most recent and most serious works in this field is by a universal man, who is mathematician, geneticist, numismatist and archaeologist. The book is *The Culture and Civilisation of Ancient India in Historical Outline* (1965) by D. D. Kosambi.

Is India a country outside history? There are few traces

of primitive Indian history, no landmarks in a past which extends for tens of thousands of years.

So far no one has been able to decipher the mysterious script that was written five thousand years ago at Mohenjo Daro in the Indus valley. The only thing that is certain is that this language of the Indus culture has nothing in common with the Indo-European tongues which are supposed to have succeeded it. Two Finnish students, the brothers Parpola, one of whom is a philologist, the other an Assyriologist, helped by a young computerologist, Seppo Koskenniemi, have been working for some years on deciphering this language, which seems to be half-way between the Chinese system of ideograms and the syllabic system of our own languages. Decipherment, which depends on the theory of a possible connection with Dravidian roots, has not yet produced satisfactory results, and the tablets have not "spoken."

An unknown people, who lived in the Indus valley in the third millennium B.C., inscribed their mysterious records on these tablets. For a few centuries, there was a civilization there as brilliant as those of Egypt and Sumer. Then came its eclipse. An undoubtedly degenerate society collapsed and disappeared abruptly. Because of floods? Because of invasions? We do not know.

During the decline of Mohenjo Daro, invaders are reputed to have set fire to the city and massacred its inhabitants. If they did, they have left no trace in history. It is thought that certain legends in Vedic literature refer to them, but this is by no means sure.

Professor Kosambi describes these invaders as the first Aryans, but admits that his point of view is controversial. He tries to identify Mohenjo Daro with the city of Narmini, which is described in the Rig Veda. Generally speaking, he accepts everything in the Vedas that he finds technologically possible at the time they refer to. He rejects everything else, even though there are texts giving exact descriptions of flying machines. It remains to be seen whether this method does not bypass a number of ques-

143

tions, some fantastic, some reasonable. The author looks on the Aryans as nomads massacring everyone who crossed their path and destroying all the cultures they encountered. Of the many wars described in the Vedas, the author considers all the ones in which technically advanced weapons play a part to be mythological. Obviously this is an academic point of view. Nevertheless, it is a very superficial point of view. If one automatically looks on every product of a technology above the average level of the period of legendary, one obviously ends up with some attractive folklore on the one hand, and a tidy, but banal history on the other.

The abundant and sometimes cranky literature inspired by *Le Matin des magiciens* has familiarized the reader with the echoes of extraterrestrial visits in the ancient sacred texts, and in the Vedas in particular. A systematic analysis of all the oral and written traditions dealing with this subject has not yet been made, but it is not the only puzzle that still awaits solution. If man is older than was believed twenty years ago; if the idea of slow progressive evolution must be called in question; if the cliché of the monkey-faced imbecile rubbing two flints together is a "nightmare of the classical archaeologist," then the cliché of a technology that stayed in the cradle for 25,000 years and suddenly started running two centuries ago to break all the speed records must be the delirious dream of the same, undoubtedly neurotic archaeologist. This hypothesis presumably stands up better to experimental control than the hypothesis of "primitive magic," which proceeds from a subjective and literary interpretation.

But, ask the classical archaeologists, if advanced techniques existed in the past, why do we find no traces of them? The answer is that we *do* find traces and perhaps we should find even more if the urge to look for them existed.

In 1930, a German engineer, who had gone to Baghdad to repair a drainage system, found a chest containing various uncatalogued "religious objects" in the cellars of the city museum. In this way, Wilhelm König discovered a battery that was two thousand years old. After John Campbell had given this find some publicity in his review *Analog* in 1938, the University of Pennsylvania acquired the strange six-inch-high object and confirmed that it was indeed a battery using iron, copper, an electrolyte and asphalt as an insulator.

Was this a forgotten technique or one that was neglected almost as soon as it was discovered? A procedure for gilding temples that no one bothered about afterwards? An instrument used by the priests to perform "miracles"? Or the vestige of knowledge and techniques the keys to which were lost, so that it was discarded out of ignorance or the inability to use it? In 1967, new discoveries were supposed to have been made in the same museum in Baghdad. Information about them is not yet available.

In 1901, an amphora dating to the second conteury B.C. was taken from the sea near the island of Antikythera in the Greek archipelago. It was sealed. When opened, it was found to contain a fairly large, badly rusted metallic object. In 1946, a new process for recuperating oxidized objects was developed in order to make use of arms and material abandoned on battlefields. In 1960, an Oxford professor, Derek de Solla Price, had the idea of using this process to examine the rusted object from the Antikythera amphora. After deoxydizing and reconstructing it, he found that it was a machine made of a special bronze obviously intended for calculating the positions of the planets in the solar system. He could not establish how old the bronze was.

Was the Greek ship that sank two thousand years ago carrying in the amphora a very ancient machine which no one knew how to use? In his book *Science since Babylon*, Derek de Solla Price thought that there was "something frightening" about this discovery and pleaded for a revision of archaeology.

\* \* \*

In 1965, Dr. Bergsoe (whose works are quoted by Kaj Birket-Smith) rediscovered a gold-plating technique that is unknown today, but was first used in Ecuador around the year 1000 and right up to the arrival of the Spaniards. The object to be gold-plated was covered with an easily smelted alloy of copper and gold. Then it was hammered and heated. The copper turned into an oxide that dissolved in a vegetable acid, the sap of the shrub *oxalis pubescens*. The layer of gold remained. This technique is simpler than the method by amalgam or electrolysis. Is it not conceivable that many things, whose realization in the past we dismiss automatically, might have been achieved by processes we know nothing of? Is our technology the only efficacious one? Nature, which yields up its secrets impartially to Marxists and capitalists alike, may have yielded them up in the "prelogical" past quite as often as in our progressive present. To reject this embarrassing theory, must we say that such technological discoveries were the result of chance? Yet in the case of gold-plating, we are faced with a complicated process with four consecutive operations.

Here is another example. The Viennese ethnologist, Robert von Heine-Geldren, has established that the techniques of bronze founding in Peru and Tonking around 2000 B.C. were so similar that they could not be the result of coincidence. He assumes that these techniques could have been brought from Tonking in south-east Asia to Peru by travellers. One would like to know how they travelled and why they took a manual of metallurgy with them. In order to economize on theories, we are inclined to postulate a common source. Questions, questions . . . But there are others that are even more disturbing and curious.

On 13 February, 1961, Mike Mikesell, Wallace Lane and Virginia Maxey were collecting geodes about 5 miles north of Olancha, California. Geodes are hollow spherical or oval stones, the insides of which are lined with crystals. The three were collecting for their shop, which sold rare stones and gifts. Sometimes the geodes contained gems which they sold. On this particular day, they found a stone which they took for a geode, although it bore traces of fossil shells. The next day they cut it in half, ruining their diamond saw in the process. In cross-section, the exceptionally hard material was like porcelain or ceramic, with a shining two-millimeter-long metallic rod in the middle.

Members of the Charles Fort Society, whose hobby is investigating strange facts and studying everything out of the ordinary, made an X-ray examination of the object enclosed in the "geode" (ceramic, copper, metallic rod), which was reminiscent of some kind of electrical equipment. The owners of the mysterious "geode" are now offering it for sale for 25,000 dollars. If this object is not enveloped in a muddy concretion, but in sedimentary stone, as seems to be the case, we are confronted with a fantastic enigma.

Naturally, we do not tell these stories with the intention of starting a revolution in archaeology. We simply want to point out that there is a host of similar questions to which no really satisfactory answer has been given. We poor amateurs who put these questions know that it is best to dream without letting dreams get the upper hand. But it is permissible to dream. It might even be that dreaming is highly recommended for research into the past, for it is the main weapon in the fight against the inky blackness of past ages. And the fight against time is the only activity worthy of the man who feels and knows that there is something eternal in him.

# 2 The Statistician in the Stone-Age Cave

When the tourist gets back into his car to visit Lascaux after a delicious lunch at some restaurant in Montignac or Les Eyzies in Périgord, it is probably because he has been following a gastronomic route taken from the Michelin guide, not because he is a culture vulture—and yet, no one goes to Montignac without visiting the caves of Lascaux. So the tourist gets out into the famous meadow, chatting as he descends the short flight of steps that terminates in the rotunda. At first, only the ground is illuminated. It takes a few minutes for the visitors to assemble round the guide. There is still nothing to be seen and they keep on talking. But suddenly the light is switched on and the paintings emerge from the shadows, red and black against the dazzling whiteness of the wall.

Then every time, the same scene is repeated. These twentieth-century men, women and children, most of whom know nothing about prehistory, to whom the words Palaeolithic, Magdalenian and cave art are double-Dutch, are all, without exception, overawed. A reverential silence falls on the group. These people, who have just been revelling in truffled foie gras, sense the fantastic presence of the men who came here 15,000 to 20,000 years ago to express in their paintings the aspirations of their minds and hearts.

What do these wonderful paintings mean? What inspired their creators? A visit to Lascaux often stimulates a thirst for knowledge that surprises the man who feels it. The fact that Lascaux has earned the name "the Sistine Chapel of prehistory" for the beauty of its paintings and that this chapel was painted so long ago poses an enormous problem to every reflective mind and we can understand the passion with which the first prehistorians once justified and defended their new science.

Jacques Boucher de Perthes fought for thirty years, from 1828 to 1859, to win recognition of the existence of the Stone-Age men he had discovered. It seems as if the passions involved in these ideological and often personal struggles have dogged prehistory right down to our own day, like original sin. Although a steady stream of finds has been made since Boucher de Perthes collected the first axes made of dressed stone near Abbeville and recognized them for what they really were, prehistorians have never quite succeeded in establishing a strictly scientific method of interpreting cave art. The stratigraphic classification of finds is an exception. When an archaeologist finds an object buried in the earth, he describes the other objects that were found at the same level, especially fossil remains of living animal and vegetable organisms. No one would dispute this description when it is properly done. Until recently, this was the only material about which scholars could publish studies without the risk of the discussion degenerating into personal squabbles. Even in the last century, when it was simply a question of dating objects found in layers which geologists had long since identified, this uncertainty was very disagreeable for the prehistorian. But starting from the first years of the twentieth century, when the authenticity of the caves decorated with paintings and engravings could no longer be denied and the problem of establishing their chronology arose, it became a torment. The fact is that the vast majority of the works of art engraved or painted on cave walls have nothing but themselves to offer the investigator. He is confronted with a painting of a bison, let us say a fresco. How is he to know whether it dates to the Solutrean or the Magdalenian? If he makes a mistake, the answer may be as much as 10,000 years out! What methods should he use?

The first real answer to this question was given in the

epoch-making work of that giant of prehistorical scholarship, the Abbé Breuil. When the Abbé began to study the French caves, about 1900, prehistoric science had already accumulated a good deal of experience. But there was a gap when it came to decorated caves. Little or nothing was known about them. The young priest, Henri Breuil, was the ideal man to investigate palaeolithic caves, endowed as he was with a tremendous capacity for work and reading, and being willing to make all the intellectual and physical efforts required of him (to reach the painted and engraved walls of underground caves, it was often necessary to crawl on one's stomach, climb or dive into icy water, etc.). He also had a brilliant flair for spotting what others had missed and was an excellent draftsman, combining creative imagination with a keen critical sense, which was feared by his adversaries. He classified the superimpositions of the drawings, he classified the different styles by their affinities, he showed how the shapes, the materials and the techniques developed, and after half a century of hard work and reflection he established the chronology of nearly all the works of this art which was created and forgotten thousands of years ago. To find another lifework like his in the human sciences, one would have to go back to Cuvier, if not to Linnaeus.

The only thing is that the very genius of the Abbé Breuil seems to emphasize the subjective nature of the science he created. For we certainly cannot impute his discoveries to a method. It was the inexhaustible well of his work and imagination that brought to light all those lost centuries. Breuil was a fantastically gifted empiricist. He produced results, but not a method. Anyone who wanted to follow in his footsteps would have to be a second Abbé Breuil.

About 1945, a young ethnologist, who was passionately interested in prehistoric art, made his appearance. He was not a pupil of the Abbé Breuil and his temperament was diametrically opposed to the Abbé's. André Leroi-Gourhan was as cold and reserved as Breuil was impetuous, as absorbed in his own thoughts and the ideas of others as Breuil was outgoing. But what the two men had in common was patience, creative imagination and scientific integrity.

About 1947, Leroi-Gourhan began to use objective methods for a chronology of prehistoric art. Year after year, he systematically studied nearly all the decorated caves inch by inch. And where Breuil had spent years underground putting thousands of sketches of engravings and painting on paper, Leroi-Gourhan also spent years measuring, classifying and counting. Gradually, for the first time, numerical data were added to Breuil's irreplaceable sketches.

"The material I have used," he writes, "consists of 2,188 animal figures distributed among 66 decorated caves or rock shelters which I have studied *in situ* . . . In order of frequency, I have counted 610 horses, 510 bison, 205 mammoths, 176 ibexes, 137 bovidae, 135 hinds, 112 deer, 84 reindeer, 36 bears, 29 lions, 15 rhinoceroses, 8 giant deer, 3 beasts of prey, 2 wild boars, 2 chamoix, 6 birds, 8 fish and 9 monsters."

But while the statistical data were accumulating in the files, the image of a certain absolutely consistent arrangement of animals and signs in the caves was gradually impressing itself on the mind of the methodical scholar.

The recognition of a specific arrangement of painted motifs throws a new light on our ancestors of 20,000 or 30,000 years ago. It means that we must stop regarding them as savage magicians obsessed by the game they had to kill, or as primitive men dancing round their hunting totems. We find that they seem more worthy of our respect and that they pose questions about the workings of the human mind in the remote past. For there is no doubt that we are dealing with a creative power which is infinitely nobler, stronger, subtler and more abstract than the clamor for food for the tribe. And this will clear up a contradiction which ought to have been worrying us for a long time—the contradiction between the consummate art of the drawings and the simple meaning which ethnography hitherto attributed to them.

The results achieved by Leroi-Gourhan's objective statistical cataloguing of the cave pictures call in question all our previous conceptions of prehistoric art.

In 1879, de Santualo claimed that the cave of Altamira near Santander in Spain concealed paintings executed by Stone-Age men. The prehistorians split their sides with laughter. They went on laughing for twenty years. Then Abbé Breuil and Carthailhac went to investigate the matter and the laughter changed to stupefaction. These frescoes really were the work of men who had lived in the Palaeolithic and from the aesthetic point of view they were just as good as modern paintings.

Stupefaction is not a scientific attitude and scholars abhor this feeling. And since more and more cave paintings were discovered every year, it became all the more urgent to find confirmation that Altamira was not just a historically unimportant exception. It turned out that the caves, and for preference the deep caves that lay in eternal darkness, played a vital role in the psychology of our remote ancestors. Ethnography, a science that was still in its infancy at the time, supplied the explanation. Because scholars had noticed that twentieth-century primitive men practiced hunting magic, danced in front of animal figures in order to cast spells on them, because they pierced drawings of antelopes and zebus with lines representing arrows, it was assumed that Palaeolithic man had done the same. And so pressing was the need for an explanation (the more harmless, the better) that this supposition was immediately accepted. Some scholars did object that the same primitive people who currently practice hunting magic also practice war magic, and that we know prehistoric skulls that obviously show signs of violence, in other words that our ancestors fought each other, and yet we find hardly anything in the caves but animals. But now that an explanation was at hand, it was not going to be given up because of trivial objections. That is why for half a century the convenient and reassuring theory of the poor savage, still little better than an animal, dancing in the depths of his cave in front of a painted bison in the belief that he was preparing his victory over a charging bison has not ceased to drone in our ears.

It did not seem to worry anyone, least of all the prehistorians, that Spain was the ideal terrain for ethnography where one had only to seek a little to find proof of one's preconceived theory, while believing that it was a discovery. Anyone who cast doubts on the validity of hunting magic in the presence of the mammoths at Rouffignac or the deer at la Pasiega was simply raving.

So when Leroi-Gourhan looked for a way to penetrate into the soul of Palaeolithic man, he took great care to avoid easy explanations such as "the cross between Eskimos and Australians." Not because he rejected an ethnographical explanation *a priori*, but because he refused to pack this ready-made explanation in his baggage.

The method he used was based on the statistical analysis of 72 groups of cave pictures. He carried out his studies in 66 caves, which represented nearly the whole of European cave art (there are 110 decorated sites altogether, but the 44 which Leroi-Gourhan excluded contain few works of art). What was the end result of these statistical calculations? It was simply to demolish the theory of hunting magic and reveal the men of the last glaciation as beings as complex as ourselves.

To begin with, we shall let the figures speak for themselves. 91 per cent of the bison, 92 per cent of the bovidae and 86 per cent of the horses are depicted in the central composition of decorated caves. In the other parts of the caves, these animals are scarcely found at all. Inversely, the central composition contains only 8 per cent of the hinds, 20 per cent of the reindeer, 9 per cent of the deer, 4 per cent of the ibexes, 8 per cent of the bears and 11 per cent of the felines found in the whole of the same caves.

In other words, these percentages show that certain

153

animals are nearly always found in the central composition and that others are virtually never found there. Why? Once the statistician had come to this conclusion, he could theorize as to the reason. Perhaps Palaeolithic man had a marked preference for bison and bovidae, or perhaps these animals were the most numerous (which, incidentally, is disproved by fossil remains). But a hardheaded statistician refuses to theorize. He sticks to his method, which consists in letting proven facts speak for themselves. Like his colleagues, Leroi-Gourhan had noticed that the cave walls were often dotted with special signs, which were always remarkably similar, in addition to the animal representations. These signs have stimulated endless speculation. Some scholars think they are more or less schematic objects, others that they were signposts to guide visitors to the caves, yet others that they are meaningless doodles or even the artists' signatures.

To begin with, Leroi-Gourhan confined himself to arranging the signs typologically and discovered in the process that they all derive from a few original shapes. Essentially, they are the phallus, the vulva and the profile of a naked woman. In other words, there are male and female signs.

Whereabouts in the cave are the signs? Here again it was only necessary to count them. The figures obtained (we omit the detailed percentages, because of the great number of signs) show that nearly all the female signs appear on the central composition (or in the cave's lateral cavities), whereas only 34 per cent of the male signs are found there.

So the Palaeolithic decorated caves have sectors with male symbols and others with female symbols. And as the same animals are generally depicted in the same places, the animal world as a whole is divided into a vast bisexual zoogony. Male animals appear at the entrance, male and female animals in the center, male animals at the back of the cave. From the very earliest period, human figures were symbolized by the graphically simplified representation of the organs of reproduction. But at various periods there are complete representations of men and women.

The analysis of the topographical and sexual symbolism can be carried much further. The cave basically comprises six zones, each of which has its own meaning; the central composition, the side caves, the ambulatory, the entrance, the "passages" and the back or end of the cave. It is striking that the representations of the human hand, mostly made in the form of a "negative" by applying the hand to the wall and blowing liquid color round it or dabbing the color round it with a pad, are nearly all found at the entrance to the cave and on the central composition, and that nearly all the female signs that are not on the central composition and in the side caves are found coupled with male signs at the entrance.

What does all this mean? Looked at objectively, it means that the decorated cave is divided up according to some unknown metaphysical system, the symbolism of which is just as exacting as Christian metaphysics. Just as a Catholic church in principle contains twelve columns representing the twelve apostles, just as the pictures of the Stations of the Cross always go in the same order from the left of the altar to the entrance, then from the entrance to the right of the altar, the decorated prehistoric cave, too, follows a figurative arrangement that is remarkably constant from one end to the other of the vast area in western Europe where the caves are found and during the thousands of years when they were used.

Admittedly there are variations in this arrangement. Local and temporal variations, just as today we speak of Perpendicular and Romanesque. But the general arrangement remains true to the concept of a world divided into two sexes. Certain characteristics that are suggestive, but sometimes difficult to interpret, indicate that the cave itself was considered as a vast natural symbol of the female stomach. For example, the narrow passages are often daubed with red, and the part of the cave allotted to the female animals is very often painted with abstract male signs, or with hands, as if to indicate ownership, or the presence of men. Lastly, as we have seen, the entrance and rear wall of the cave are frequently reserved for male symbols. But an explanation which relies exclusively on the universe of sex and fertility is not enough.

We look at these wonderful drawings and engravings, we do not feel for a moment that we are in the presence of suggestive or lascivious art. The celebrated "pregnant animals" of classical ethnography are neither more nor less "sexual" than the stallions of Chinese paintings, with their massive members, and nowhere in cave art does sex appear to be reproduced for the sake of sex. This art is apparently dominated by the act of reproduction, but its special characteristic is its exceptional modesty, its predilection for symbols and abstraction. Whereas abstract sexual signs are present everywhere, these cave men never once drew a couple having intercourse! The few men who are depicted in a state of erection (ithyphallic, as the prehistorians call them, with traditional puritanism) are drawn without realism. Generally even, like the celebrated ithyphallic corpse in the well at Lascaux, they have animal features emphasizing their symbolical nature.

If the significance of this art was not sex for sex's sake, nor sex for fertility's sake, what was it? What kind of a metaphysic emerges from all this symbolism? Let us admit, says Leroi-Gourhan, that we have no idea. Let us admit the paucity of our knowledge and accept the fact that these men who lived twenty or thirty thousand years ago have left us the undecipherable writing of a subtle and complicated idea, whose deeper meaning we can only guess at. But the very fact of discovering that it is writing, which is to some extent comparable with the writing contained in the art of the cathedrals, and of having achieved this by the scientific method of objective calculation, leads us to hope that we shall be able to decipher it one day. Then we shall lose the "primitive" men and find our brothers in the abysses of time. Then we shall know who these metaphysicians were who possessed such wonderful artistic techniques and penetrated into the depths of the earth to perpetuate the symbols of their spiritual life there.

# 3   The Unknown Men of Australia

Separated from Asia before *homo sapiens* appeared (according to the classical chronology), Australia is a dry, mainly flat continent, whose surface area is about the same as the United States. Mountains and rivers are concentrated in the east, but you can go from the Gulf of Carpentaria in the north-east to the south coast through stony deserts and flat dusty areas of vegetation, without ever rising above 600 ft. However, traces of salt pans and rivers that dried up thousands of years ago indicate that this continent enjoyed a milder climate towards the end of the Pleistocene or at the beginning of the post-glacial age, and that the arid expanses that now teem with ants were once green.

Did the first inhabitants come from those distant ages? How and why did they come? Was Australia a penal colony even in prehistoric days? Was a part of the human race brought here to live in a "reserve" on this gigantic island, which has no mammals and no wild beasts and is populated solely by marsupials and strange jumping herbivores? When white men landed in 1788 to put their convicts ashore in this lunar landscape, they found no traces of temples or pyramids, no trace of an ancient civilization; all they found was 300,000 nomadic aborigines—one human being per square mile in the valleys of the east and near the coast, one per thirty or forty square miles elsewhere. And in spite of all the difference between the humid regions and the vast expanse of arid land, they had made no particular adaptation to their environment. They were ignorant of agriculture and lived solely by hunting, fishing and food gathering.

The mystery of these silent lands produces strange

dreams. The science-fiction writer, Erle Cox, imagined a golden sphere buried deep in the Australian earth in which slept a man and a woman, who had belonged to a long vanished culture. Lovecraft dreamt of underground libraries and laboratories that had been abandoned by extraterrestrial visitors. From 1929 onwards, a little archaeology took the place of such fantasy. Later, perhaps, archaeology on a much larger scale will restore fantasy to its rightful place.

There are few peoples as poor as the first inhabitants of Australia were. There were no animals with horns or tusks to supply material to make weapons with; very little flint or fine-grained stone—a lot of quartz and that was all. There was no trace of tombs or dwellings; no pottery, no metals, no precious stones; no remains of culture and no bones of domestic animals, with the exception of the dingo dog. Where did the dingo come from? How long has he been the aborigine's companion? Excavations made during the last few years by J. D. Mulvaney at Fromm's Landing date the dingo's appearance to about the third millennium B.C. And it was the dingo, in company with human hunters, that wiped out many animal species, such as the "Tasmanian wolf." For millions of years, the only changes in the ecology were caused by the hunger of the dingo and the hunger of men, hunting and setting fire to things.

But until 1960, it was thought that the first settlement of Australia had taken place not long before the arrival of the convicts, three thousand years earlier at the most. In 1929, Hale and Tyndale made the first archaeological discoveries in the valley of the Murray river (Adelaide). On a site sheltered by cliffs, they excavated a layer of twenty feet of stratified deposits. At the deepest part of the deposit, they found the points of stone projectiles, above them short bones pointed at both ends, which may have been hooks, and at the surface primitive utensils of bone and stone like those still used by the aborigines today.

Radio carbon tests showed that the lowest layer dated to approximately 3000 B.C.

By and large, and until Mulvaney's researches during the last decade, scholars followed Tyndale and Hale's theory that there had been three cultures: the stone tool culture, the bone tool culture and that of the modern aborigines who used both stone and bone. During these three thousand years, there had been various immigrations, because there had been various "cultures." (There has been no trace of migration to Australia to support this supposition.)

Between 1960 and 1964, Mulvaney excavated in a rock shelter in South Queensland (Keniff Cave) that contained 11 ft. of deposits. He dug up 850 dressed stone projectiles or scrapers, the majority made of quartzite. Carbon 14 dating made them 16,000 years old. Further excavations at Sydney, in the Northern Territory, at Victoria and in South Australia enabled Mulvaney to advance a more convincing theory than Hale and Tyndale's, that there had not been any different "cultures" and immigrations, but a development which was characterized not by the transition from stone to bone, but by the transition from tools without handles to tools with handles. For 11,000 years, the inhabitants of Australia did not know about the handle. Handles or shafts, resin for attaching them and the remains of thongs and cords of gut and hair are first found in the layers dating to about 3000 years ago. In other words, there was a remarkable period of stagnation lasting more than 10,000 years, followed by abrupt technological progress, which was accelerated in the last thousand years when we see the emergence of more finely worked stone tools, knives and scrapers, scissor blades and gouges, as if a "ban" had been lifted and man had freed himself from some taboo or destiny.

What do we know about this man? There is a good deal of information, including collections of oral traditions, assembled by the first European colonists. Nevertheless, the legends, customs and beginnings of technology observed with varying degrees of accuracy do not really provide the elements for an interpretation of the prehistoric past. When should we date the appearance of the first men in Australia?

In 1940, a human skull was excavated from the gravel quarries at Keilor, near Melbourne. A carbon 14 test carried out on a piece of charcoal found nearby gave a date of just under 16,000 years. In 1965, a well-preserved skeleton was found in the same district and the dating was the same: 16,000 years. The discovery of human fossils is an extremely rare occurrence. A last indication was supplied by comparison with the skulls found at Wadjak and Sarawak on the island of Java that are reputed to be 40,000 years old.

When we think how vast the continent is and how small the number of human fossils excavated, not to mention how recently excavations began, we can understand Mulvaney's rather melancholy caution when he says: "We shall have to dig a lot more to fill in the gaps in our knowledge and come to generally valid conclusions."

Yet in Australia, like everywhere else in the world, modern science is constantly pushing the origins of human history several thousands of years further back. Today we can imagine that the unknown men came in masses when the climate was most favorable, when there were broad flowing rivers, when lakes full of fish were surrounded by luxuriant vegetation and when gigantic herbivorous marsupials supplied the immigrants with food, but dangerous beasts of prey were non-existent. By what searoute did this immigration take place? For what reason? Was it the exodus of a whole race? The formation of a "reserve" on a continent with no hidden dangers? Fear of some peril to which mankind was exposed? Did they arrive in an ark? Was it an experiment performed by superior beings? Did they choose this gigantic uninhabited territory to deposit their knowledge in? Were enormous masses of workers brought there to bury this knowledge? Worker commandos in the dream sands of kangaroo land?

* * *

But although scholars are helped in Australia by the descendants of the first aborigines, their oral traditions and knowledge of their places of refuge, it is not so in Tasmania, the island which is separated from the mainland by the Bass Strait. The white men completely exterminated the original Tasmanians. By the end of the nineteenth century, not one of them was left. We are cut off from any source of information. Excavations have yielded projectiles of dressed quartz, but there is not a trace of tools with handles. How did men originally cross the Bass Strait? Studies of the sea bed indicate that Tasmania was connected with the mainland in the Pleistocene. Yet the map of Australian and Tasmanian prehistory remains a vast silence. There is nothing to explain this isolation and the remarkable technological and cultural stagnation. And lastly, there is nothing to imply that the first Australians came from New Guinea, for the difference between the cultural levels of the two populations is considerable.

Discovered five hundred years ago, the island of New Guinea, which is still one of the least explored regions of the world, is partially administered by Australia today. There is strict segregation of whites and natives. The administrator in Port Moresby rules over bays full of stones, empty bottles and rotten hulks inhabited by natives who have sold themselves for the lowest wages in the world. The old men who have come from the forest and ended up here wander drunkenly through the streets. Apathetic women sit on the ground and try to sell lemons, betel nuts and necklaces of seashells. The Murray barracks, an enclave surrounded by barbed wire, dominates the center of the town. The administrator in chief, who has not forgotten the hard days of tribal warfare and the general insecurity, asserts that the country is not ready for independence and maintains the same repressive attitude as when there were cannibals (in fact, some still exist) and headhunters. He is an ultra-conservative former racehorse trainer and farmer from Queensland and ethnology is not exactly his hobby. His assistant is a former male nurse. There have been few changes in the country. Tribes have been pacified and territories opened up that were completely wild twenty years ago. Missionaries and doctors have been at work. In the face of considerable resistance, a small native élite has formed, consisting of five hundred students at the university, but it is unpopular. The old colonial spirit has not changed. Its "blessings" are dubious, and accepting an intelligent young man "so that he can learn our language and take the benefits of civilization back to the natives" means at best that he is made an officer's "boy."

Contacts with the tribes that live in the forest have been of little use to the white men, who do not understand their language and are indifferent to their special human and cultural qualities. The natives are "rock apes" or simply "Oli" to the administrators. This word means "anyone" in pidgin English. If independence comes quickly, hastened by anger and misunderstanding, without sufficient social training and organization of a people who have been treated contemptuously so far, the streaming forest will close again over its mysteries. The tribes will forget the brief sojourn of the white men and renew their relationship with eternity. With their hair dressed like a Napoleonic two-cornered hat, shaken by chronic coughs, they will move through the white mists in the clayey valleys of the highlands and roast the bodies of the last missionaries—deserving though they may have been— wrapped in banana leaves on red-hot stones. But perhaps the young men who will be responsible for the country, although facing greater difficulties, will be able to understand their brothers better than the Australians and reveal their souls to us. Of course, they will return to their forests and their magic, and they will start to hunt the bird of paradise again (which can only be killed with a lance or an arrow, because guns are taboo for this beautiful bird)—these Papuans, who only came to hear the administrator's speech, because he was opening the new landing strip at Koroba. They came, their bodies smeared with lard or white mud, one with a ball-point pen in his nose, another stark naked, with a zip-fastener round his forehead and the little boy, who wore nothing but a pair of painted glasses.

Unlike Australia, where the cultural status of the natives stagnated at a primitive level, the subtlety and multiplicity of the culture of New Guinea are astonishing. The different tribes live in valleys which are difficult of access and there is very little communication between them. But all these valleys are bubbling with activity. Five hundred different languages are spoken, i.e. a tenth of all the languages spoken in the world, and some of them prove to be quite elaborate. The Duna language, for example, which divides living creatures into categories (those which fly, those which walk and the low ones, those which crawl— the last-named including women and pigs), has an extensive vocabulary, the variations of which are tonal, like Chinese. Clothing, ornaments, mores and traditions are extremely varied among a people that does not know the concept of unity, yet is undoubtedly the most egalitarian and independent on our planet. With no sovereigns or hereditary leaders, they only choose a chief in case of hostilities, so that he can lead them in battle.

It seems as if the men of New Guinea make it a point of honor to adhere to their customs, and far from wanting to ape the whites, they emphasize their singularity passionately and with a sort of laughing gaiety. The best known of the young leaders of New Guinea, Leo Hannett, who was educated at a Catholic missionary school and then at the university, admires Camus, Martin Luther King, Kennedy and Senghor. If he were to take over the government of his country one day, he would try to stop his brothers becoming deracinated by emigration to cold artificial towns. He would like custom and tradition to be intimately linked in the genuine country, in the small villages and in the clearings where the sweet potato is cultivated.

What kind of dialogue could be established between the intellectually curious and abstract thinking white men, worshippers of concrete and diagrams, and these men originating from country that Salvador Dali might have painted, men who paint flowers on their legs and adorn their heads with bird of paradise- or parrot-feathers? Ten years ago, the white men organized an exhibition of farm animals and agricultural machinery at Mount Hagen. The natives heard about it and came out of the jungle to visit it, clad in their holiday costumes. There were so many of them that at the next fair they stole the show from the Australian and Dutch farmers by organizing a unique and fantastic "biennial of prehistory." Since then, they come every 2 years, in August, to show the whites and themselves what they are like. Tribes that before knew nothing about each other assemble, dance, sing, utter war cries and brandish lances and bows and arrows. There are 20,000 of them in the arena; the earth shakes and the tourists with their cameras get trampled on. The Assaros, the Kandeps, the Chimbuns, the Hewas and the Laiagaps have walked day and night through valleys in which explorers normally meet less than a hundred men on a journey lasting several weeks. There are the Porgaigas, with their wigs decorated with gold buttons, wearing necklaces of dogs' teeth and loincloths made of shells. There are the Dunas who live in huts. Their men and women are kept separate; they only meet in the bush. They paint their faces yellow and red for their initiation ceremonies and pull through their nasal septums blue feathers so long that the ends reach their shoulders. There are—and they are the strangest and most staggering—the little men from the river Asaro, smeared all over with gray and ochre mud, wearing big masks made of the same mud, primordial, uncouth, terrifying and suffering figures.

But of course tractors and prize-winning cows must be sold too. At night, the organizers of this white fair chase these thousands of witnesses to magical eternity away, so that the Minister can make his speech, the army march past and the enthusiasts play polo.

Why this exuberance in New Guinea and the stagnation in Australia? There do not appear to have been any contacts between the two. The myths of east Australia relate that the earth gradually emerged from a primordial sea, but say nothing of visitors or travellers. They all begin with the "ages of the dream," eternally present and sources of all life, the reign of the heroic celestial creators, fathers of shamanism, who lived in heaven in a place which was filled with cool water and quartz crystals. These were the gods who ruled over procreation and death, both of which were supernatural. Another hero, sometimes wise, sometimes foolish, was the mediator between gods and men. He transmitted the rudiments of knowledge, technology and magic medicine. Running through all these myths, there seems to be a taboo on change and evasion, as if the endless expanses of Australia were really a sort of penal colony for these men.

In 1963, a strange and disconcerting piece of information reached us from Australia. A pile of Egyptian coins that had been buried about 4,000 years ago was found in terrain sheltered by rocks. The readers who gave us this information referred to some rather obscure reviews, for there was no mention of this find in archaeological publications. However, the widely-read Soviet review *Tekhnika Molodezi*, which devotes a regular column to unexplained facts with comments on them by experts, took up the matter. It even published photographs of the excavated coins. If this find is confirmed, although archaeologists are bound to treat it very skeptically, all kinds of questions arise.

Knowing the type of ships which were available 4,000 years ago, we cannot imagine an Egyptian expedition to Australia. And that brings us back to our theory. Was this continent a depository, a safe, roomy hiding-place for visitors from afar, or a prison for a specific race, which was deported there and kept in a state of ignorance? That is obviously nothing more than a romantic question to add to the mystery of when Australia was originally populated. Scholars had thought that it was quite a recent phenomenon, but a small number of excavations made during the last ten years now push the date back to the Palaeolithic. In the meantime, we wait for more systematic research to reveal the secrets of this country which has been forgotten by time.

# 4  Communication between the Worlds

One July morning in 1911, a farmer, a Peruvian soldier and a young professor from Yale University called Hiram Bingham were walking over a frail bridge of sticks and lianas which led across an abyss between gigantic blocks of stone. In the bottom of the abyss, the waters of the Urubamba rushed to meet the Amazon. While the three men were continuing their climb on the other side of the bridge, clinging on to the trees which grew on the precipitous slopes, they discovered a series of terraces surmounted by a labyrinth of wonderful pale granite ruins. Beneath a covering of vegetation, they could see the fantastic nameless citadel, which was dominated by the terrifying peaks of the Huayna Picchu and the Machu Picchu.

From that day on, Bingham, a fighter pilot in the First World War and later Senator for Connecticut, clung passionately to his interpretation of the origins of the mysterious citadel of Machu Picchu until his death in 1965. He firmly believed that it was the Tampu Tocco mentioned by the Spanish priest Fernando Montesinos in his *History of Peru Before the Conquest*. Montesinos was the first historian to write about the Peruvians and he was responsible for the first studies of the mineralogical resources of the Andes. He died in 1562. According to Father Montesinos, long before the Incas, the dynasty of the Amautas governed the Andes, and during the reign of the sixty-second Amauta barbarian hordes invaded the empire. In the year 800, soldiers of the defeated army carried their king's corpse to a refuge called Tampu

168

Tocco. This refuge was turned into a citadel, from which an Amauta, Manco Capac, stormed down in 1300 to seize Cuzco and found the Inca Empire.

It is a controversial theory. The existence of Manco Capac has not been proved. He may have been a legendary hero, or perhaps Manco Capac was the symbolic name of a dynasty of rulers who lived before the Incas. According to oral tradition, Manco Capac came from Tiahuanaco. So we are directed to another ruined city in the mysterious prehistoric past. Between 1200 and 400 B.C., the Chavin civilization flourished on the plateau of northern Peru and left behind vestiges of a work of art abounding in ferocious gods. On the same sites, scholars have found the traces of prehistoric master-builders who erected pyramids and colossal fortresses made of blocks of sun-baked clay. The most astonishing of these monuments still stand at Tiahuanaco, south-east of Lake Titicaca. Acres and acres of ground are covered with truncated pyramids, artificial hills, lines of monoliths, platforms, underground rooms and gates formed of two pillars and a lintel carved from hard stone. The famous Gate of the Sun, with its inscriptions, is said to suggest an astronomical calendar. Was this site the center of an empire, as Machu Picchu was? And if these lofty wind-lashed uncultivable sites, the ages of which cannot be established, were not used as living centers, what were their functions? And what was the nature of the Nazca culture, on the north coast of Peru? Older than the kingdom of Chimu, which has left us the imposing ruins of Chanchan, the Nazca culture, the origin of which is unknown, has left on the desert plains, on the sand and gravel, gigantic geometrical figures, and outlines of birds, whales and spiders, the lines of which are more than four miles long, and which seem to have been drawn so that they could best be deciphered from very high up in the sky.

Nazca remains an enigma. In his fine book *Ancient Ruins and Archaeology*, Sprague de Camp writes: "As the people of Tiahuanaco, like the other vanished South

American civilizations, had no written tradition, there are no inscriptions waiting to be deciphered. There is nothing to help us retrace the lost history of Tiahuanaco. Events which cannot be written down are obliterated for ever when those who remember them die. That is why the history of the Inca fortress of Machu Picchu, and the enigma of the lost empire of Tiahuanaco, are very likely to remain unsolved for ever in the mists which swirl around the towering peaks of the Andes."

Here we must return briefly to the theories of Hanns Hörbiger, to which we referred in our book *Le Matin des magiciens*. As we know, Hörbiger, who had his moment of fame under the Nazis, believed that man was already civilized in the Tertiary era. According to the Austrian amateur cosmologist's "cosmic ice" theory, before our present-day moon existed, six satellites formed by exploding stars were attracted and destroyed by our earth in different geological ages. When the satellite approached, it disintegrated in the atmosphere and its fragments were scattered over our planet. The Flood and Atlantis are fitted into this framework. According to Hörbiger, the "moon" of the Tertiary era crashed 20,000 years ago. All the tropical countries were submerged, except for some high mountains, in Peru and Ethiopia, for example. In the opinion of Hörbigerians such as the Inca experts, Hans Bellamy and Arthur Posnansky, Tiahuanaco and Machu Picchu date from this period. They were refuges for the élite of the Tertiary era and were just above sea-level at the time.

Perhaps there are clues to be followed up among these fantasies, but Hörbiger's claims have been demolished by too many recent astronomical observations for us to adopt them. So we shall limit ourselves to making a rapid zig-zag trip through South America to deal with some questions based on studies and discoveries that are wholly or partially verifiable.

\* \* \*

The chronicles tell us that about 1526 B.C., the Inca Huayna Capac, "the living god, son of the Sun," learned that strange men with pale faces had been seen off the northern coasts of his empire in unusually shaped ships of abnormal size. In fact, Pizarro did land on the coast of Ecuador in 1532 and travel southwards through the Inca empire. But what Huayna Capac was told about palefaces had a long tradition behind it, telling of white men who came from the sea in "the night of time." Father Montesinos even asserted that the Peruvians were descended from Ophir, Noah's great-grandson.

The first proof of a sensationally early contact between South America and the Mediterranean culture was discovered quite recently. Professor Cyrus H. Gordon, who teaches archaeology at Brandeis University in Waltham, Massachusetts, believes that he has deciphered a Phoenician message on a rock in the Brazilian province of Paraiba. This rock inscription was first discovered in 1872, but scholars concluded that it was a forgery, because the grammar did not tally with what was known of Phoenician writing at the time. Since then, many inscriptions with the same style have been found in the Near East. There no longer seems to be any doubt about its authenticity, at least as far as Gordon is concerned. He points out that Phoenician ships were more solidly built than Columbus's and had circumnavigated Africa on several occasions. So why should they not have reached Brazil, too?

This is the text:

"We are the sons of Canaan and come from Sidon, the city of the king. In search of trade, we were driven shore in this distant mountainous country. In this nineteenth year of Hiram, the great king, we have sacrificed a young man in honor of the all-powerful gods and goddesses. We sailed from Ezeon Geber in the Red Sea, with ten ships. We sailed the seas together for two years around the land of Ham. We were separated from the rest of the fleet by a storm and we are trying to find our companions again. Thus we arrived, twelve men and three women, in

171

a land which I take possession of as admiral. May the great gods and the goddesses of power grant us their favor!"

Naturally, we should like to know what became of these Phoenicians when they penetrated inland and whether the Indian legends of white gods did not stem from their landing. If we postulate that there was a link between the Mediterranean peoples and South America, the whole interpretation of pre-Columbian history would have to be reexamined. And we should have this possibility to dream about. When these Phoenicians or their descendants travelled through the mysterious new continent, did they encounter cultures older and greater than their own? What were the repercussions? And shall we not find traces of other encounters in the past of these peoples about whom we still know so little?

Once we raise the question of contacts forgotten by history, a whole series of discoveries and observations suddenly combine to form a single challenging puzzle.

Along the whole length of the Amazon, pottery is found that dates to at least 2000 B.C. It has a recurrent motif of entwined snakes very similar to those on ancient Near Eastern pottery.

The language of the Mahua Indians has features that are identical with the Semitic tongues. The language of the Quechuas resembles Turkish.

The association of Venus with the entwined snakes is found in both the Mexican *Codex Borgia* and Near Eastern inscriptions, especially at Ras Shamra.

The Aryan god of light, Mithras, has a snake lying at his feet. The *Codex Troano* tells us that in Mexico the beam of divine light stood vertically upright with a snake at its foot. In Bolivia, scholars have found the same snake, and also inscriptions reminiscent of the Near East and men wearing turbans. The bas-relief at Itaquatiara de Inga in Brazil is covered with inscriptions resembling those of the Near East.

More than two thousand coincidences between ancient Egyptian words and Brazilian inscriptions have been found, which led C. W. Ceram to say: "The older languages are, the more they resemble each other, thus proving that they all derive from one mother tongue."

Systematic study of the monument at Itaquatiara shows not only a connection with the Near East, but also elements in common with Easter Island, Mohenjo Daro and Harappa. A common origin? The general consensus of opinion is that the monument was engraved 20,000 or 30,000 years ago. What do we find on this bas-relief? Phallic symbols, mandalas in the form of multiple flowers curiously resembling Indian mandalas. A recurrent symbol is reminiscent of the figure eight: two snakes, or a double infinity.

Lastly, can we establish links between Itaquatiara de Inga, the Marcahuasi culture discovered by Daniel Ruzo and the Nazca culture studied by Maria Reich?

Another culture has just been found by the Peruvian engineer, Augusto Cardich. It is very high up in the Andes, near Lake Lauricocha, and must be at least 13,000 years old.

If there were mighty cultures in South America, if they made contact with the outside world through visits from the Near East, then the mystery of South America may be the most extraordinary of all those dealt with in this book.

Important vestiges of the techniques of ancient cultures were still extant a century after the discovery of America and they excited so much curiosity that Benvenuto Cellini went to Mexico to try to learn how the Andean artists made silver fish with gold scales. Undoubtedly they refused to give him the information, because he returned to Italy post-haste.

Metal objects dating to at least 500 B.C., as well as decorative techniques using pulverized precious stones and cinnabar, have been found in Peru.

About the time of Christ, smelting was already known

173

in Colombia and platinum was worked in Ecuador. The Dane Paul Bergsoe has proved that the Ecuadorians were familiar with powder metallurgy.

As from 1000 B.C., the craftsmen of Colombia, Panama and Costa Rica made casts with the lost wax process. Recently, some extremely beautiful bird heads cast by this process have been found in Panama. Soldering was well known and metal thread was manufactured by extrusion. The origin of these techniques seems to have been in the Andes, but this only pushed the problem further back into the past. Even if the Phoenicians actually arrived in Brazil, they could not have taught techniques which they did not know themselves.

A strikingly modern installation for extracting and treating copper ore has been excavated at Cobres, in north-west Argentina. Objects were also made there, one of the most interesting being an ornament made of animal and bird figures assembled in the manner of Arcimboldo.

Lastly, we should mention that the Uraeus, the symbol of power of the Egyptian Pharaohs, is also found among the Campos Indians of the Andes. Until the end of the eighteenth century, linguists claimed that Egyptian was the original language of mankind. Today we must ask whether their studies were not underestimated in the following century.

Now let us take a look at South America's connections on the Pacific side. Today it has been proved that the Japanese landed at Valdivia (Chile) about 4,000 years ago.

If cultures that possessed elaborate techniques and were aesthetically and intellectually advanced existed in those millennia—and everything points to that conclusion—and if these cultures themselves were the scattered remnants of much older cultures, such as Tiahuanaco, they must have been informed on several occasions of the existence of a world beyond the great ocean and they must have incorporated this information into their world in some way Professor Marcel F. Homet is undoubtedly right when he says: "One indisputable fact emerges. A wonderful culture of which we know nothing flourished in the past in South America."

But perhaps we shall know something about it one day, for the spirit of adventure is not dead yet and there are more countries hiding mysteries than we think. Disillusionment is the product of ignorance, not knowledge. The man who wants to know will discover that each of his footsteps treads the surface of deep mines in which slumber the power and knowledge of vanished worlds. Everything is still kept secret, from the Ireland of the Celtic Numinor to strangely silent Australia, from Lascaux to Easter Island, from the Gobi desert to Amazonas.

Explorers have always claimed that an unknown culture still exists in the unexplored jungles of Amazonas, or more precisely in the region bounded by the Rio Xingu, the Rio Tapajos and the Amazon. The city of "Z" of this persistent romantic dream is supposed to be located at latitude 19° 30' south and longitude 12° 30' west. In the strange notebook of Colonel Percy H. Fawcett, who disappeared in this region in 1925 without a trace, we read: "The answer to the problem of the origin of the American Indians and of the prehistoric world will be given when the ancient cities of the Solar culture are rediscovered and opened up to scientific research. For I know that these cities still exist." In fact, Indians had told Fawcett about a city that was still living, inhabited and illuminated at night. But no one has ever set foot on this *terra prohibida*.

Like Colonel Fawcett, Alpheus Hyatt was an extra-ordinary example of the romantic explorer. He died in 1964 at the age of ninety-three, after he had written nearly a hundred books about Central and South America. He never tried to penetrate the *terra prohibida*, because he was convinced that he would die there. But he writes that he was allowed to consult the secret archives of the Duke of Medinacelli, which, so he says, contained the charts used by Columbus. These charts not only showed the outlines of the two Americas, but also gave details of the interior. Verrill, and his widow after him, never wavered in his conviction that highly developed cultures had existed in South America and that important vestiges of them still remained. As the majority of Verrill's predictions, especially about Phoenician inscriptions and the chemical methods used by the ancient Peruvians to work granite, have been verified, his most obstinate claim deserves to be treated with some respect.

In memory of Colonel Fawcett and Verrill, we add two pieces of information. They are not of vital importance, but they came into our possession during the last few years. The first was supplied by Miguel Cahen, one of the directors of Magnesita S.A., in Brazil, which is interested in industrial ores and in particular in the by-products of magnesium which are used in metallurgy. One of the company's prospectors found a strange crystal on the borders of the *terra prohibida*. Miguel Cahen sent it to Jacques Bergier. Examination of the crystal showed that it consisted of exceptionally transparent magnesium carbonate, with very remarkable properties in the infrared spectrum, and that it polarized these radiations. No crystal of this type is described in mineralogy. Bergier sent the crystal to the Office national de Recherches aéronautiques français (French National Institute for Aeronautical Research). The specialists declared that the crystal could only be of artificial origin. That is how the matter stands at present, for Magnesita S.A. did not have any other specimens.

The second piece of information reached us via a Brazilian journalist, Cecilia Pajak, of the Newspaper *O Globo*. According to her, about 1958, a certain number of German war criminals who had fled to Brazil were due to be extradited. Some of them sought refuge in the *terra prohibida*. Usually, people who crossed into this zone disappeared for ever. But these Nazis were an exception. Since 1964, their families residing in Brazil have been receiving letters posted in the interior. The letters state that these men are prisoners, but are well treated. They are not allowed to say whose prisoners they are . . . Are they hostages in some secret city from the remote past, about which Colonel Fawcett spoke with such conviction?

# 5 About Ancient Chinese Science

Intellectual contact with China is by no means easy. Even if we know the language, it is still difficult to grasp the arguments and views of those we are talking to. While we were writing this book, the European physicists of the European Nuclear Research Agency in Geneva were discussing the following problem. Did the recent Chinese discoveries about "statons" constitute a tremendous advance or were they simply known facts worded in Chinese cultural language? American physicists were equally puzzled. So we shall make Professor Tchi Pen Lao of the University of Peking and the New China Agency responsible for their own statements. According to these sources, granite bas-reliefs representing non-human beings, or rather male divers with elephants' trunks (breathing apparatuses?) have been discovered in the mountains of Hunan, as well as on an island in Lake Tung Ting. These beings were depicted either upright on land or on the surface of cylindrical objects floating in the sky. According to the same sources, the bas-reliefs are 45,000 years old! This does not contradict our theories, but all the same we should like to know how this dating was established. There are various methods for fixing dates when carbon 14 cannot be used, such as thermo-luminescence and palaeomagnetism. However, as far as we know, these methods have never been used *in situ* and as the Academy of Science in Peking does not answer letters, it is difficult to form a judgment. Let us hope the information is accurate and mention in passing that Chinese myths frequently allude to extraterrestrial visits.

178

The oldest authentic documents and objects that can be used to establish and prove the idea of a science and a technology in China date, in fact, from the first three centuries of the Christian era. Between minus 40,000 and plus 300 there is a considerable distance in time, the longest we have so far mentioned in this book.

Objects made of aluminum bronze have been found in tombs dating to the second century A.D. Of course, that is impossible, but the fact remains. Aluminum bronze cannot be made without electrolysis, yet the Chinese alchemists made it. How did they go about it? That is what we would like to know. In any case, it is interesting to clarify some details about Chinese alchemy. We have used the UNESCO *History of the Ancient World* (Part III, English edition). Chinese alchemy, whose roots go back to the very remote past, was aimed at transforming the adept by making him acquire bodily immortality and wisdom, but the manufacture of gold by a traditional process of transmutation was a stage on the way to obtaining products that would enable the adept to transcend the human condition. As the UNESCO history makes clear, alchemic gold was not meant to be sold.

The first known alchemic text is the Ts'an-t'ung-ch'i. Like all the secret masters, the author wrote under a pseudonym. In ninety paragraphs, the text explains how to make the pill of immortality by a complicated thermal treatment in a hermetically sealed egg-shaped recipient. As in the famous *Book of Changes*, the treatise uses the binary language of modern computers. The terms Yang and Yin, the dualism which is the basis of the doctrine of Taoism, can already be found in it.

A certain number of alchemic treatises have been rediscovered, all from the first three centuries A.D., but referring to much older facts. The authors believe that the alchemists who have successfully accomplished the Great Work are still living on "an island of immortals." Let us get down to what can be proved.

There are two indisputable sources about Chinese

179

science. One is the book by Dr. Alexander Kovda, director of UNESCO's department of exact and natural sciences. The other is the monumental history of science in China by the English historian Joseph Needham, published by the Cambridge University Press.

The first undisputed fact to emerge is surprising. The Chinese had a highly developed and accurate knowledge of seismology. This is something quite unique in the history of ancient civilizations. It was the Chinese who drew up an exhaustive list of earthquakes. It begins in 780 B.C. and continues until A.D. 1644. The chronicles say that the gods who came from heaven demanded that this list be made. Thus the gods took a particular interest in the structure of the terrestrial globe. But there are stranger things to come. Chang Heng, who was born in 78 and died in 139, invented the seismograph. His apparatus consisted of a bronze vessel with a domed cover containing a central column (essentially a pendulum). The latter could move laterally along tracks in eight directions and work a closing and opening mechanism. On the outside of the apparatus, there were eight dragons' heads, each holding a bronze ball. Below each head, a toad with open mouth was ready to receive the ball should it fall. With the data provided in this way, it was possible to find the epicenter of an earthquake, using a ruler and compass. There can be no doubt about the existence of this apparatus, but perhaps there has not been enough reflection about its possible interpretation. Within the framework of Chinese arts and customs at that period, it implies the application of advanced scientific principles and postulates a knowledge of the earth's structure, of mathematics and even of the propagation of waves, the origin of which is unknown. Every trace of this kind of research vanished after the Han dynasty. Why?

Kovda's book also contains interesting facts about Chinese astronomy, which preceded alchemy and was the secret lore of the priest kings of the Chu dynasty. They were partly mythical and partly historical, and historians disagree about which Chu emperors were real and which were not. For example, the Emperor Yao is sometimes called mythical and sometimes historical. He is supposed to have given high offices to astronomers, though once again we do not know whether they were real people or legendary figures. Very little of this secret lore has reached the west. It is supposed to have concentrated in the study of a planet that was invisible, yet in the solar system. As from the fourteenth century B.C., we note the systematic observation of eclipses of the sun, which seem very ancient even for those days, going back to dates which it is hard to accept because they refer to tens of thousands of years in the past. We should know more about them if we possessed written documents, but a great number of them were destroyed during the cultural revolution, not Mao's cultural revolution, but Wang Mang's. Wang Mang, nicknamed the Usurper, ruled China from A.D. 9 to A.D. 22. He introduced special reforms, but imposed such harsh taxes on the country that he was assassinated in the winter of the year 22. A large number of texts disappeared during the revolt.

We first find documents towards the end of the second century A.D., nearly 200 years later. They contain a theory, which in turn drew on an immemorial tradition, that the cosmos is not composed of matter and that the stars and planets are floating in endless empty space. This theory is very close to the modern view and is absolutely unique for that period. As from A.D. 5, there were also machines which imitated the universe, following a star in its orbit and making it possible to predict eclipses. In the third century, the prediction of eclipses was already very accurate. At the end of the fourth century, the Chinese had reached the stage of being able to predict whether an eclipse of the sun would be total or partial. All this is clearly confirmed by the studies of Joseph Needham and Alexander Kovda. Thus heavenly clockwork (the expression is Joseph Needham's) seems to have been absolutely original. It differs from contemporary experiments in Alexandria and from later apparatuses in Europe in its system of coordinates, which is based on declination and the ecliptic. The Chinese apparatuses are far more reminiscent of modern telescopes than of the mechanisms of the ancient Greeks or even those of the European Middle Ages.

If we look at things from our point of view, we must admit that we have to do with a secret science that developed very differently from astronomical research in Europe. We should also point out that magnetism was known as from the first century A.D. It was used for orientation, although the compass was not invented until a century later. But spoon-shaped magnets bearing a picture of Ursa Major and oriented to the south are described as from the first century A.D. They are also reputed to be incredibly old, dating back to the age of immortal alchemists about which we know nothing.

These researches seem to be connected with advanced mathematics and closely linked to Taoist magic. In the second century A.D., we find the *Memoirs on the Traditions of the Mathematical Art,* which links the secrets of numbers with the Taoist mysteries.

On the practical level, the heirs of the mathematical tradition invented the abacus around the time of Christ. Unlike other inventions, it did not reach the west where it was discovered independently.

All the descriptions of scientific development in the first millennium B.C. refer to magic mirrors. Some of these mirrors are still supposed to exist in private collections. We do not understand how they were made or what they were used for. They are mirrors which have extremely complicated high reliefs on the back of the looking-glass. When direct sunlight falls on the mirror, the high reliefs, which are separated from the surface by a reflecting glass, become visible. This does not happen in artificial light. The phenomenon is scientifically inexplicable.

Other properties are attributed to these mirrors. If they are set up in pairs, they transmit images, like television.

To the best of our knowledge, no experiment checking this has been made. The UNESCO specialists explain that the properties of these mirrors are due to "small differences in curvature" (?) and are rather reticent about their other properties. If it were possible to prove that these mirrors contained printed circuits and formed a method of communication, the existence of advanced technology in ancient China would be proved.

Lastly, in our view, a final and essential proof of the existence of a higher science in ancient China is provided by the *I Ching*. It would take several volumes the size of this book to explain the significance of the *I Ching* in detail. Here we shall only mention what we consider essential, pointing out in passing that C. G. Jung's work on the subject is of paramount importance.

What is the *I Ching?* The *I Ching,* or *Book of Changes,* is a book in which all the situations in which a human being can find himself are methodically enumerated. It is also an oracle which enables anyone to find out exactly what his situation is at the moment he consults the oracle. The coding which makes these revelations possible is so old (possibly four thousand years) that it is impossible to establish its age. It is based on the binary system, like computers. This "apparatus for self-knowledge" apparently functions in conjunction with paranormal phenomena. As in the parapsychological experiments of the American psychologists Rhine and Soal, there is a violation of the law of probabilities and a kind of bridgehead between the past and the future. It is indisputable that the oracle answers and that most of its answers are sensible. If a fraction of the money spent on trivial, but reassuring research had been devoted to the *I Ching,* universal knowledge would certainly have been advanced.

The interesting thing, apart from the paranormal aspect of the phenomenon, is the use of a binary code and also the subtle classification of all human problems into a limited number of typical situations. This implies abstract thinking that was certainly equal to or higher than that of any known culture in 2000 B.C. And if we recapitulate Chinese achievements—the manufacture of aluminum, seismography, astronomy and cosmology, the synthesis of gold, magic mirrors and the *I Ching*—we realize that there was an absolutely original culture in China and that it was wholly technically oriented.

This culture obviously raises many questions about the past, but it also raises some about the present. If the Chinese had a tremendous capacity for abstraction allied to considerable technical ability from the most remote past, why did not China rapidly dominate the world? Why did the West win the victory over this mighty culture?

The traditionalists explain it by saying that Taoism rapidly degenerated into charlatanism and that the link with the "immortals" was broken. The materialists, such as Joseph Needham and Alexander Kovda, say that the proletariat let itself be enslaved and that China missed the chance of the industrial revolution and an October 1917.

None of these answers is entirely satisfactory. But if we want to understand the pride of contemporary China, we must go back to the ancient sources and seek there the reasons for an immemorial self-respect and an immemorial justification for the ambition to rule the world.

# 6   A Trip round Numinor

Numinor, the Atlantic of the north, the Celtic Atlantis, is not nearly so famous as Atlantis itself. Yet the name still evokes some literary echoes in Anglo-Saxon countries, because it has been used as a basis for two widely-read imaginative trilogies: *Out of the Silent Planet,* by C. S. Lewis and *The Lord of the Rings,* by J. R. R. Tolkien. Yet even to anyone who has read these wonderful books Numinor remains the vague symbol of a center around which early Nordic culture was concentrated.

We do not even know the geographical position of this center, but if we take the sagas seriously, it seems very probable that the Celts must have had their Athens or their Rome. We know nothing of its foundation or its fall. Was it a mythical city from the next world? How can we be sure? We can examine the history of ancient Ireland for traces of Numinor, but we shall not find any. Nevertheless, we are going to do so, for Ireland's history has come down to us in symbolical form, and to comprehend it, we have to psychoanalyze it, so to speak.

After the universal Flood, the island that later became Ireland was first ruled over by the queen and sorceress Cesair (a reincarnation of Circe). Cesair and all her people perished. About 2640 B.C., Prince Partolan, who came from Greece, landed in Ireland with twenty-four men and twenty-four women. Ireland originally consisted of a single plain, with three lakes and nine rivers, but Partolan enlarged it and afterwards it had four plains and seven new lakes. Partolan's companions multiplied. In 300 years, there were five thousand of them, but a mysterious epidemic destroyed them all on the Feast of Beltin. Their communal grave is on the Hill of Tallaght,

185

near Dublin. However, around 2600 B.C., the race of the "Sons of Nemed" (their name means sacred), who came from Scythia, landed on the island, which they thought was uninhabited. Another group of invaders landed there about 2400 B.C., on the day of Lugnasad (1 August), the third great feast of the Celtic year. Most of them belonged to the Fir Bolg (Belgian Men?), others were called Gaileoin (Gauls?) and Fir Domman (Dummonnii from Great Britain?). Lastly, the Tuatha Dé Danann, of divine origin, came from the "Western Isles," where they studied magic. They brought their talismans with them. Nuada's sword, Lug's lance, Dagda's cauldron and Fal's "Stone of Destiny," which cried out when the legitimate king of Ireland sat on it. These successive invaders all had to fight the race of monstrous giants that originally populated Ireland. Some of them had "only one foot, one eye and one hand," others had the heads of animals, usually goats.

These monsters were the Fomoiri. A war broke out between the Tuatha Dé Danann and the Fir Bolg. The first battle was fought at Moytura (Mag Tuireadh, the "Plain of the Pillars," i.e. of menhirs), near Cong, in present-day County Mayo. The Tuatha Dé Danann were the victors. During the battle, their king Nuada lost his right hand. The skillful healer Diancécht—the Irish god of healing—replaced the lost hand by an artificial silver one, but Nuada "of the silver hand" was forced to abdicate. He was replaced by Bres ("the handsome"), son of Elatha ("the wise one"), king of the Fomoiri, and of the goddess Dé Danann Eriu (unknown goddess of Ireland). The two hostile races formed marriage alliances. Bres married Brigit, the daughter of Dagda, while Cian, son of Diancécht, married Ehniu, daughter of Balor "of the evil eyes." But Bres was a loathsome tyrant. He burdened the country with taxes and forced labor; he scorned Caïrbre, son of Ogma, the greatest bard of the Dé Danann. Bres had to abdicate after seven years and then Nuada acceded to the throne again, for his real hand had been rejoined to his wrist through the skill and incantations of Miach, another of Diancécht's sons. For this, Miach incurred his father's jealousy and was killed by him.

However, Bres held a secret council in his submarine abode. He persuaded the Fomoiri to help him to drive the Dé Danann out of Ireland. The preparations for war took seven years. During this time, Lug the infant prodigy, "master of all the arts," grew up. Lug organized the resistance of the Dé Danann, while Goibniu, the god of handicrafts, forged weapons for them and Diancécht made a miraculous spring gush forth that healed wounds and revived dead warriors. But the spies of the Fomoiri found this spring and rendered it useless by piling bewitched stones on it. After a few duels and skirmishes, a great battle took place in the Moytura of the north (plain of Carrowmore, near Sligo). In the course of the desperate struggle, many heroes were killed. Balor "of the evil eye" slew Nuada with his death-dealing look. Then Lug put both Balor's eyes out with his magic sling. Reduced in numbers and demoralized, the Fomoiri retreated and were driven into the sea. Bres was taken prisoner and the dominion of the giants over the island was broken.

Yet the power of the Dé Danann was to undergo a rapid decline. Two gods from the empire of the dead, Ith and Bilé, who landed at the mouth of the Kenmare, intervened in the political councils of the victors. Mil, son of Bilé, rejoned his father in Ireland, accompanied by his eight sons and their retinues. They arrived on 1st May, just like the first invaders. On the way to Tara, they met three goddesses in turn: Banba, Fodla and Eriu. Each of them asked the Druid Amergin, Mil's soothsayer, to name the island after her. The island was finally called Erinn (genitive of Eriu), because she had been the last to ask. After further bloody battles, in the last of which Manannan, son of the sea-god Ilyr (ocean), intervened, the Tuatha kings were slain by the three surviving sons of Mil. A peace treaty was concluded, the Tuathas renounced the isle of Erinn and withdrew to the country of the beyond. All they asked in return was that a religious cult be devoted to them and sacrifices made in their memory. That is how religion is supposed to have started in Ireland.

All this is myth. However, "we ought not to consider myth as a stupid piece of 'fabulization' by the human mind at grips with Pascal's famous deceitful powers, but rather as an operational technique with the same epistemological value as mathematics. Then we might understand the lessons of history better, for history is bursting with myths that dare not speak their names. We should understand the Celts and their intellectual attitude." (Jean Markale.) So it is through myth that we shall try to reach Numinor.

The way is long. Let us begin at the beginning. In Celtic mythology, we find an accurate and perfectly rational chronology which is based on the two inseparable principles of life and death, both of them associated with the earth, as foster-mother. Man goes through three stages on earth: birth, life and death. On a Celtic medal, each of these stages is represented by a horse's head. The three heads are absolutely identical, indicating a kind of fusion between the stages.

Water is closely connected with the ground (and the underground). It is the liquid element mixed with the telluric element and the sacred properties of these elements resemble each other. At first there were no animals in the land and the soil yielded scanty nourishment. But "a solitary one" received a visit from spirits who came from elsewhere. They counselled him to descend to the mother of marine animals. He followed their advice and dived into the water. When he came back, he brought game with him, not fish (a curious fact), and at the same time he brought joy as a present for his fellow-men.

The Celtic god of food, Aryaman (etymologically the protector of the Aryas, or Indo-Europeans), plays a dual role, rather like the ancient Roman god, Janus. He also exists in ancient Persian Mazdaism. But his ambivalent aspect—his beneficence as opposed to the terror he sometimes inspires—is absent from the Persian cult. In the Persian religion, two forces are opposed: the spirit of Good, Ahura Mazda, and the spirit of Evil, Ahriman, who also represents the power of darkness. This opposition is also found in their art, especially on the façades of buildings, where architects combined effects of light and shade, with the help of reliefs and hollows. Many Achaemenid monuments testify to this. We can easily imagine that the buildings of Numinor had the same characteristics.

But another element, the moon, whose cult is attested in the most ancient legends, is associated with water and earth. Like all the peoples of antiquity, the Celts did not worship the moon for its own sake, but for the part it played in all forms of life. Firstly, it had an influence on the growth of plant life, then on women's menstrual periods and lastly on tides. Moreover, the Celts first acquired accurate concepts of time and measurement from the phases of its waxing and waning.

So the first religions were connected with our planet and its satellite, and water played a special part in them. Immersion in water "symbolizes a return to the unformed stage," emergence from water, the cosmogenic gesture of creation.

Because of this constant interaction, the dark underground world, which originally inspired an understandable terror, gradually lost its odium, for the kingdom of the dead is also Mag Mell, the happy plain of the Elysian Fields, and Tir na n'og, the land of youth. But as from a certain moment which cannot be established, the underground and marine gods were replaced by others who came from outer space. It may be that this substitution marks an upheaval, a conquest. The invaders are the sons of Mil, who conquered the Tuatha Dé Danann. They had enjoyed tremendous power for thirty centuries. To form some idea of their might, we have only to look at the granite fortresses and walls on the coasts of Ireland which have been "melted" to a depth of 1 ft. by a weapon with effects remarkably like those of a laser or of thermonuclear fusion.

Their departure was connected with a crime, as in the myth of the Judaeo-Christian Fall (and perhaps in the myth of the disappearance of Numinor). The crime was supposed to have been committed by Morigana (demon of the night), daughter of Boann (the eternal) or Ernmas (the murderer), also called Bodb (the crow). However that may be, the gods of the sun weighed the balance in favor of fire and consequently (from another aspect) of death.

In fact, although in the great cultures of Greece and Asia the sun always assumes the preeminent role of fertilizing creator and symbolizes the victory of mind over matter, its setting is associated with decline and disappearance, so that although it engenders man, it also devours him. Nevertheless, Lug, the most important Celtic sun god, mainly plays a beneficient role and has outstanding qualities. He is the undisputed master of the arts of peace and war. He is styled Sahildanach (literally, polytechnician, smith, carpenter, poet, warrior, historian, magician). He embodies all the highest activities of the tribe. He possesses a magic lance, which, of its own accord, strikes down the enemy who threatens the god. His bow is the rainbow and the Milky Way is called Lug's Caine in Ireland. The radiance of his countenance is such that no one can look him in the face and this recalls the phenomenon called the Glory of the Lord in the Bible and "the great galaxies" in science-fiction novels. He also has some of Mercury's features, and we should not forget the disastrous effects of brightness and heat in many Greek myths, including that of Icarus.

Dagda cannot compare with Lug, but he fascinates men as god of music. On his magic harp he plays in turn the melodies of sleep, laughter and sadness, and his listeners sleep, laugh and weep. This is rather reminiscent of the effects of certain musical themes in India. Some of them even have the power to kill those who hear them if they are played at a certain time.

After the sons of Mil had tamed the destructive fire and turned it into a beneficient power, a peace treaty seems to have been concluded between them and the underground gods. The latter took refuge in the gloomy regions in the center of the earth, but left them at regular intervals, returning to the surface and taking part in men's lives, visibly or invisibly, but always tangibly.

However, the Celts are still waiting (if not exactly for a redeemer or a Messiah) for a predestined being, Galaad, who will indicate the exact meaning of each action, so that the functions are regenerated. For the world of the "sacred" is ambiguous. If each thing, by definition, has a fixed nature, a force, on the contrary, engenders good or evil, depending on the orientation which it assumes or which is given to it.

When we consider how much importance the Celts attributed to myths, we realize that they were not simply fables. They represent everything that is just the opposite of the Logos of the Greeks and the Historia of the Romans. According to the Christians, they are beliefs which are not justified by the Holy Scriptures and consequently without any foundation, but one could retort that very few events seem to justify the Holy Scriptures.

For a very long time, the myths were handed down orally from generation to generation. The oldest Irish texts, which form the basis of their folklore, date to the fifth century B.C., although some enthusiasts would like to date them much further back. Admittedly, it has not been proved that there were no Breton manuscripts, but they must have been dispersed during the Norman invasions. It is plausible that these manuscripts written in a barbarian tongue which no one outside the peninsula understood were thrown away or destroyed after they had come into the possession of the monasteries.

191

We do not know exactly how far back these legends go. Their origin is lost in the mists of Indo-European and autochthonous prehistory (most of the extant texts are written in Gaelic or Welsh).

The last form taken by the Celtic myths is the cycle of Arthur and the Round Table. Even in this late form, the symbolism remains obscure, and in addition Christian morality has often added heterogeneous elements to the pagan legends. The latter are wrapped in mystery on principle; they are meant to be esoteric. "The common people should never have access to knowledge," said Taliesin, the legendary sixth-century Welsh bard. Some manuscripts were put in a safe place, either to prevent them from coming into the hands of the common people, or to preserve them from the ravages of invaders or thieves. From time to time we hear of a "hiding-place" or a stock of manuscripts that have been brought to light by chance or after intensive research.

One of the authors of this book came close to finding one of these hiding-places when he was enquiring into the cult of Alkar-az at Rennes in 1938, but in the end he was refused access to it. During the last few centuries, many scholars have tried to interpret the extensive Celtic literature. Some specialists, including Georges Dottin, have devoted several books to the analysis of the texts, and literary and historical commentaries on them.

Many writers who have been inspired by the Celtic legends, Numinor, for example, have distorted them badly. Distortions of this kind were probably made because the study of this culture, which preceded the arrival of the Greeks in Western Europe and the Roman conquest, was neglected for a very long time. For centuries, inveterate Hellenists and Latinists tried either to deny altogether that the conquered peoples had made any contribution to mythology, or to minimize their genuine merits and the importance of the problems which have grown even more obscure in the course of two thousand years. Historians despised the inhabitants of Ireland to such an extent that they frequently confused them with the Cimbrians, who have a completely different origin, even though they interbred with both the Celts and the Teutons.

This conspiracy still continues today, so that there will be no risk of tarnishing the brilliance of the culture diffused in Gaul by Julius Caesar and his successors, and also by the Christian evangelists. Fortunately, especially since the nineteenth century, unprejudiced scholars have tried to make at least a partial reconstruction of the civilization which entitles us to believe in the existence of Numinor, and to determine exactly where it was located. According to Eugène Pittard, who is nevertheless extremely cautious and adduces the theories of Broca and Dieterle, the cradle of the Celtic peoples was located between the Harz and the Bohemian-Moravian highlands. About the beginning of the second millennium B.C., the Celts emigrated and split into groups. After several centuries, one group reached Asia Minor, where the Greek colonists called them Galatians (hence the name of a suburb of Istanbul—Galata). The new arrivals also founded the small town of Ancira, modern Ankara, in the heart of Anatolia.

But for reasons already mentioned, their achievements and contributions to culture in this region have been belittled or completely ignored. When classical authors did mention the Gaelic invaders of Italy and Delhi, they mainly emphasized their savagery, which struck terror into the indigenous population—as if autochthonous peoples have not always been frightened when foreigners, whether civilized or barbarian, invaded their country.

Between 950 and 700 B.C., in the Hallstatt or early Iron Age, a Celtic tribe set off from the Harz and fanned out westwards. One group settled in Gaul, another passed through Holland, Belgium and the Seine basin, reaching first Scotland, then Ireland.

The exact origin of the Celts has long been a subject of discussion. It could be that the region between the

Harz and the forest of Bohemia was only the gathering point of a nucleus which came from elsewhere.

In view of this dissemination and the interbreeding that took place in this vast melting-pot, the characteristics of the Celtic race cannot be established with certainty. They were brachycephalic, but this feature diminished in the course of centuries of crossbreeding with the indigenous peoples they came across in Scandinavia, the Iberian peninsula, Italy, Bessarabia, Poland, etc.

About 5000 B.C., we come across a legend rather like the story of the Akpallus. According to the myth, the Fomoiri (*fo* = under; *mor* = large and sea; i.e. telluric and Atlantic power) were warriors. With one foot, one arm and one eye, the head of a goat, a horse or a bull, they were reptile-like demons who were already settled in Ireland when the first invaders came. Each new wave of invaders, whether sea- or air-borne, clashed with them, without being able to wipe them out. This is the Akpallus all over again, but without their diving-suits.

Their language rapidly split into two groups: the Celtic, or Gaelic, and the Cymric. Gaelic was mainly spoken in the Scottish highlands and Ireland, forming two dialects which gradually began to differ from each other. But in spite of the distance, we find many of their roots in pahlavi and even in modern Persian.

In the first centuries of the Christian era, the Celts used the writing called Ogam, which was based on the Latin alphabet and consisted of perpendicular and oblique dashes above and below a straight line. Later they mostly used the Latin alphabet. But although doubts have been cast on their culture, their military organization was highly respected. Their cavalry, their chariots, their fortified camps and above all their iron sabers terrified their opponents around 1000 B.C. However, military organization of that kind postulates a technology. To judge by the contempt with which historians have treated them, the Celts made no contributions whatsoever to the sciences or technology. That is odd, to say the least. A UNESCO history states that the horses of the Celtic armies were shod with horseshoes from the beginning. The mass production of horseshoes in quantities of tens of thousands naturally presupposes a whole industry, about which we should like to know a lot more. It is true that the village of La Tène, the center of Celtic culture, was discovered, but this village, which dates to 500 B.C., i.e. 2000 years after the time we are interested in, is situated on Lake Neuenburg in Switzerland. It is unlikely that it is the place where we should look for Numinor, which appears to have been a seaport. Apparently, the Celtic civilization, instead of degenerating, disappeared mysteriously into the darkness from which it had come. Because of its iron technology and powerful military organization, scholars have had to credit it with a certain cultural status, and it is known as the "western Hallstatt Culture." After this, the Celtic influence made itself felt in other countries and left its mark on the La Tène culture, which, as already mentioned, was located in Switzerland.

But before this, the Celts, like all the inhabitants of Europe, had gone through a difficult period. During the post-glacial era, the country was covered with forests in which wild bears lived. In this hostile environment, they still could not practice agriculture, which requires some security. So they stayed at the stage of hunting and food collecting for some time. One of the outstanding characteristics of their way of life was horse-taming. In the same way that they later used iron to shoe horses, they substituted metal tools for their primitive stone and flint tools. But they still continued to work flint mines. Well preserved examples of such mines have been found at Spiennes (Belgium). They were more than 30 ft. deep, with galleries like narrow tubes, through which a man with his tools could only just wriggle.

The metallurgic skill of the Celts is attested by the numerous forges that have been found in Gaul, especially in Lorraine, Burgundy and Brittany, and also by the iron cables which they used for anchoring their ships at a time when the Romans were still using hemp lines. Their smiths knew processes which made their weapons extremely hard. They also knew how to work silver.

Now all these activities suggest an organized society, i.e. urban centers or at least large-sized townships. The stage of mud huts had obviously been passed. After the lacustrian settlements of houses built on stilts, there must have been cities near the big necropolises, to which the megalithic monuments bear witness. They are all found around the North Sea, the Atlantic Ocean and in Central Europe.

R. Grosjean, an investigator at the Centre National de la recherche scientifique (National Center for Scientific Research), has found the remains of very ancient constructions, which may date to the second millennium B.C., at Filitosa in Corsica.

And the tenons and mortices that have been observed on the raised stones, especially at Stonehenge, indicate that the Celts had architectural skills and must have built stone houses. They were expert in several minor arts; they made pottery and wove rich cloths for their vestments. We must also remember that the use of amber (the "electron" of the Greeks) was known from the Baltic to the Mediterranean. The Celts worked this fossil resin, which was the sap of some form of matter immersed in water, according to Tacitus. They made it into ornaments, but they also prized amber as a means of prophylaxis. They thought that it immunized people against certain illnesses and possessed certain therapeutic properties.

Techniques were handed down orally, like the myths, and were probably the prerogative of the priesthood. This consisted of a kind of guild of natural and spiritual philosophers: the Druids. Although none of their doctrines and nothing about their activities was recorded in writing, we know about them from the accounts of several Latin authors, including Diogenes Laertius, Julius Caesar,

Strabo, Tacitus and Pliny the Elder. In addition, we have information about them from some of the lives of the saints, and, of course, from the Celtic sagas.

Their brotherhood seems to have related to that of the maguses of the Zoroastrian religion, and also a little like that of believers in the Vedic dogmas. This is not surprising when we remember that Celts, Persians and Indian Aryans all belong to the great Indo-European linguistic and cultural family. The Greek branch, on the contrary, which had amalgamated and blended its beliefs with the cultural base provided by the Cretans, differed from these tribes, as did the Romans, who were simultaneously pupils of the Greeks and heirs of the Etruscans.

So the originality of the Druids consisted mainly in their worship of nature and their ceremonial, which was linked with the seasons. Moreover, according to the Romans, they had no temples, but assembled the faithful in clearings in the forests.

They were greatly venerated. The king was forbidden to speak before his Druid had spoken. Druids served their sovereigns as political advisers, acted as tutors to young noblemen and practiced medicine based on the curative effects of certain plants. They were assisted in their ceremonial functions by the bards, singers of liturgical hymns in praise of famous heroes. In addition, they had occult powers. It is said that they performed miracles, when in communication with the spiritual powers from the beyond. They believed in the immortality of the soul and the transmigration of souls, and they prophesied, although this may also have been the function of the druidesses, about whom little is known. Soothsayers and sacrificial priests also assisted them. But sacrifice was not the same as immolation, as is often believed. It took place with the consent of the chosen person and was even sought for as a privilege. According to Jean Markale, it was "a psychic operation, in the course of which the person sacrificed freed himself by successive stages from the

197

shackles which bound him, and tried to become one with the divinity again: the perfect being."

In general, we have only an indirect idea of their store of knowledge and their customs. However, several of their customs have been preserved down to the present day, especially some of their feast days that have been adopted by Christianity. This applies to All Souls, the spring holiday, which was much earlier than our 1 May, however, and also to the feast of St. John, or midsummer night. We might say the same of certain Christmas customs. At this time in winter, it was the Celts' custom to decorate their houses, especially the entrances, with mistletoe to invoke the gods of prosperity. More than 1,500 years after the Romans had forbidden Druidism (especially after they were converted to Christianity), the Germans learnt about tradition, which had persisted in many regions, such as Alsace. However, in many places where mistletoe was scarce, it was replaced by a fir tree or a pine tree. Soon this custom spread throughout Europe and immigrants even took it to America. Today it has reached Asia and even in Mohammedan homes they illuminate Christmas trees that are laden with presents, without attaching any religious significance to them. In fact, the custom is strictly profane and is only tolerated by Christianity.

All this seems to take us a long way from Numinor. However, in order to make credible the existence of a town, which has left no trace, but the splendor of which was hymned in legend, we had to give some evidence of the cultural, artistic and intellectual level of Celtic society to show that its existence was at least probable.

An attempt has been made to link the name of this town with the rather similar name of "Numinoë," but it only appeared long after the Celtic period. Here we give the history of Numinoë so that we can refute this attempt.

In A.D. 824, Duke Louis the Pious appointed the Count of Vannes, who was called Numinoë, Duke of Brittany and leader of the Bretons.

At first Numinoë remained loyal to Louis the Pious, at least in appearance. But when the latter's sons began to quarrel about the empire, he seized the opportunity to establish full sovereignty over the region which had been delegated to him. He took the place of Lothair, who could do little against him as the rightful feudal lord, because he lived far away in the south-east of the Frankish empire. In doing so, Numinoë openly challenged Charles the Bald, Lothair's brother. Charles led an expedition against him in order to bring him to reason and take definitive possession of the Breton peninsula. But he was out of luck. On 22 November 845, he was defeated at Ballon, south of Rennes, and forced to recognize Numinoë's authority over Brittany. Numinoë then proceeded to consolidate his favorable position. He seized the cities of Rennes and Nantes, and annexed the province of Marche. In this way he established the frontiers of the future duchy, which are those of the five Breton departments today. Puffed up by his success, Numinoë became a conqueror. He fell on the neighboring provinces of Anjou, Maine and Vendômois. He died in battle on 7 March, 851, and was buried in the Abbey of Saint-Saveur de Redon, which was founded under his patronage by Conwoion, archdeacon of Vannes, and which became one of the most brilliant abbeys in Brittany.

Before he died, Numinoë had had time to trace the broad lines of political, religious and administrative reform. As he himself came from Vannes, he transferred the seat of government there from Nantes. He reorganized the northern dioceses, defining their boundaries and taking away some of their privileges in the process. He purged the traditionally Gallo-Roman clergy of the south of Brittany and tried to make the whole Breton church recognize the authority of Tours, proposing the creation of a new archiepiscopal (and Breton) seat at Dol.

There was genuine grandeur and merit in Numinoë's personality. He was one of the few Breton sovereigns to achieve the complete union of a country whose inhabitants bothered little about unity and who, as in the times of the Gauls and the insular Bretons, were torn by internal strife and struggles for precedence of the kind which form an inseparable part of the Celtic mentality. But his unity was not to last for long. There is no doubt that Numinoë was the supreme Celtic leader of the period, with an authority that was recognized by all and a name that sounds very like Numinor.

Instead of bothering further about the assonance between their names, it seems more logical to consider the vanished towns that are mentioned in Celtic literature, even though none of them bear the name of Numinor. Incidentally, their disappearances coincide with natural catastrophes. About 1200 B.C., the level of the seas, lakes and marshes of Europe was lowered, owing to long periods of drought. But at the end of the Bronze Age or first Hallstatt period (about 530 B.C.), another climatic change began. As a result of torrential rains which caused floods, the coasts of the North Sea were partially inundated and with them several ports in the Baltic, Brittany, Wales and Ireland. This entitles us to give credence to the Breton legend of the town of Ys. Admittedly, this legend has come down to us with the romantic elements which are part and parcel of the mediaeval tradition by way of the epic poem *Graelent-Meur* (attributed to the poetess Marie de France) and the *Mystère de Saint-Gwendolé*, a sixteenth-century Breton mystery play.

Yet not everything in these two tales is myth and symbol. During a sojourn in a distant land, Gradlon, King of Cornwall, had married a fairy of incredible beauty. On the return journey, she gave birth to a daughter, Dahuit, also known as Ahès, and died immediately afterwards. The widower bestowed all his affection on Dahuit, but he was converted to Christianity, whereas Dahuit remained a heathen and so that she could live away from the court, she asked her father to build her a town on low ground near the sea. He granted her wish and even protected the town with a dyke, which had a gate of bronze.

Albertus Magnus locates the town in the Bay of Douarnenez. According to legend, it was a kind of Sodom and the inhabitants indulged in continual orgies. God finally gave Gwendolé the task of punishing them. The saint warned Gradlon, the just and pious king, who just had time to save his belongings and flee. But Dahuit and her debauched companions perished. They drowned when the town sank into the waters of the Atlantic.

A similar legend is found in Wales, in the *Black Book of Carmarthen*, and another in Ireland, in the manuscripts of *Leabhar na hUidre*. There are several variations of both works, and of others that refer to cities that disappeared without a trace. In many manuscripts, it was not a tidal wave, but a magic fountain overflowing that engulfed the city. In others, a monster played a part. The same theme recurs in Scandinavia. For example, in *Nils Holgersson*, Selma Lagerlöf relates how the inhabitants of Vineta, who lived in luxury and riot, were punished. Their city was submerged by the waves, but once every hundred years, it rose again for one night. Epic literature, too, abounds with stories in which a deserted city appears to an army and then disappears mysteriously when they have surrounded it ready for a siege. Or a city vanishes when a visitor approaches it, as happened to the seekers of the Holy Grail in *Parzival*.

Of course, these disappearance can be interpreted in many different ways. The Christians interpreted the submersion of these towns as a punishment similar to that inflicted on Sodom and Gomorrah in the Old Testament. But it can also be interpreted as a personal decision to keep the spiritual power of the Celts secret made by the inhabitants of the town. Nevertheless, the recent discoveries of towns such as Catal Hüyük, and of the remains of Filitosa, entitle us to hope that Numinor really existed and that one day soon archaeologists, speleologists or oceanographers will rediscover it and supply irrefutable proof of the standard that the Celtic civilization had undoubtedly reached.

# PART FIVE

## About some Wonderful Semi-certainties

# 1 The Free Union of Knowing and Doing

We have ridden our question marks hard. Some of them were quite refractory. Probably we pushed some of them too hard, but we had to accept what we found at the post-houses. Yet the main thing was to keep moving. Now comes the last change of horses on our journey. We are going to choose horses of another kind, certainties instead of question marks. They are young and highly strung. We shall have to use the spurs lightly.

Academic archaeology has made great strides in Crete, and quite recently in Turkey, too. These, then, are the certainties we are going to mount and from time to time we shall spur them with some of our favorite outrageous questions. But are our questions really so outrageous? One day, perhaps, when some of the ideas and hypotheses in our books have stimulated further research, they will attain the status of a doctrine.

For example, our baggage contains an idea which we think deserves some consideration. It might even lead to a more accurate assessment of the past, and of the present, too. Watch how we shall use this idea in the following chapters when we deal with the myth of Daedalus and the refinements in the recently excavated cities of Catal Hüyük. The idea is as follows: every time that evidence of highly developed techniques in very remote times is found, people are staggered, not to mention put out. They are convinced that it cannot be true, because the putative science of the period was primitive and inaccurate. In other words, a civilization can only be technical to the extent that it is scientific. Our idea rejects this principle. That is to say, it rejects amazement and irritation in the face of traces of ancient technology. It frees the mind from the taboo that prevents people from nosing out and following such traces. We believe that there is not always and necessarily a connection between technical achievements and the state of general scientific knowledge in a given civilization. Admittedly, this way of looking at things is disconcerting. However, it seems realistic to us and, strictly speaking, just as valuable as an actual discovery, and this discovery may lead us to a better understanding of our own time and time past.

Our whole pattern of education, which was arranged and shaped by philosophers, men of letters and pedagogues, is aimed at convincing us that technology is a byproduct of science. Scholars discover the principles and technicians put them to practical use. According to this conventional pattern, all-round scientists such as Euclid, Descartes, Newton, Fresnel, Maxwell, Planck and Einstein are the originators of progress. And the great practical brains such as Archimedes, Roger Bacon, Galileo, Marconi and Edison confined themselves to drawing conclusions from the fundamental knowledge of the laws of the universe. Knowledge was always the first step, then came its practical application. But such a pattern, on which rests the whole of contemporary thought and consequently our way of judging the past, does not conform to reality. Generally, most of the great mental edifices of scientific genius have not led to a transformation of the world we live in nor have they contributed to man's dominion over nature. On the contrary, most of the stages in technical progress that led to our modern mastery of many natural phenomena were the result of discoveries without any philosophical significance. The great achievements were mostly made by men without any extensive scientific training, because they were not learned enough to realize that the achievements were impossible. The hoary belief in the unlimited potentialities of science does not conform in any way to the dynamic reality.

Man often acts before he knows the laws which will provide a full explanation of the results he has obtained. And the fact that he attributes these results to the gods does not mean that what he does is mythical. Blast furnaces were operating long before the birth of the chemical industry. In the past, a red-hot blade was plunged into the body of an enemy warrior who had been taken prisoner: It was believed that the virile qualities of the victim tempered the steel. But it was really organic nitrogen that had this effect, i.e. a technical process that had nothing to do with magic. When Faust first gives precedence to the word and then to thought, and finally decides to write: "In the beginning was the deed," his adventure begins and Mephistopheles enters, *disguised as a student*. . . . That is how men of long vanished cultures, disguised as high priests, with irrational minds and an aberrant vision of the universe, were able to achieve technical miracles beyond our comprehension. The answer lies neither in our refusal to examine their achievements nor in the mystique of paradise lost, of gods present at the origin of things and of an Atlantis that possessed absolute knowledge. And even if we go so far as to assume (a valid assumption, from our point of view) that there were visits from the "Great Galactics" in the night of time, they certainly did not communicate an untranslatable science, but rather processes, tricks and devices which have suffered various fates when tossed by the seas of oblivion, ignorance and indifference.

Now we should like to take a look at our own day. How cramped is the space for the passion for knowledge! How vast the space for the longing, and the need for savoir-faire! For how many years, indeed centuries, would our technical world continue, even if our whole science stopped tomorrow at the point it has reached and all the basic principles were forgotten.

Science intervened in technology quite late, and even then it met with resistance, for the impatience of *doing* finds it difficult to put up with the hindrance of *knowing*. Of course, knowledge of the laws of nature enables us to influence nature. So science has practical men, scientifically trained engineers, who are engaged on research. But trying to influence nature often shows that theoretical knowledge is wrong, or inadequate or simply useless. The inventor belongs to the world of action, not the world of laws. He is no enlightened mind. He is a mind fired by the will for immediate power. His inner flame drives him to succeed, regardless of what science considers to be realizable.

At the end of the nineteenth century, Simon Newcomb proved mathematically that the flight of an object that was heavier than air was a chimaera. Yet two bicycle mechanics, the brothers Wright, built an aeroplane. At the beginning of the twentieth century, Heinrich Hertz was convinced that the waves he had discovered could not be used to transmit messages over a long distance. Yet a resourceful Italian, Guglielmo Marconi, established the first wireless communications. We confuse the achievements of this special kind of mind, which sometimes swims with the current of academic teaching, sometimes against it, with science. In our own day, no sooner has the Faustian élan been revived by pure science, than it submerges and asphyxiates science in its waves. The "great scholar," an image which has shone for centuries, is an image that is already tarnished. The great scholar belongs to a species that has become very rare. Carried away by the above-mentioned waves or simply devoured by administrative duties, this type of man, who has made a quasi-religious choice in favor of pure intellect, rightly proud of his knowledge, preoccupied with general ideas, concerned about the consequences of his work, has become virtually obsolete. Incidentally, it is significant that instead of scholar, we use the term "research worker" today. This has nothing to do with modesty. The research worker belongs to a different race; he is more narrowly specialized and wholly oriented towards "doing."

So we see homogeneity of knowing and doing, science and technology, whereas there is really coexistence, superimposition and sometimes contradiction. The inner circles of experimental physicists are fond of saying that the extensive syntheses of theoretical physics are of no practical use to them. The same technicians will tell you that the most remarkable nuclear centers are mostly the triumph of inventors and "handymen," that they are composed of thousands and thousands of little tricky devices assembled by trial and error, without reference to basic theories. Of course they will admit that their field was first prospected by theoreticians whose work they cannot ignore.

Perhaps this is the greatest novelty of our century—that to be a technician, one must also be something of a scholar. This relationship is something quite new in the history of science. But this new fact cannot become a general rule. The marriage of these two mental activities, knowing and doing, is not necessarily a prerequisite for producing technological offspring. Even in our civilization, it is a very loose union, with fits of sulks, escapades and betrayals. Perhaps it would need a transformation of the human spirit like that accomplished by the Greeks twenty-five centuries ago to give birth to a new form of conquering the universe that closely united knowing and doing.

However, we carry this pattern of thought so deep within us that we like to refer to our civilization as "scientifically oriented." Actually, it is technological. It is in no way guided by the virtues of the scientific spirit. What dominates is the impulse of the demon of action. We live in societies of administrative officials and engineers, of bureaucrats and police, in which empiricism governs men and things with extremely vague and dubious justification and a conspicuous absence of logic. A society governed by science remains a Utopia. No, doing is not the wages of knowing, in any circumstances. This heresy has falsified our idea of the history of the mind.

The Renaissance, for example, was not a fruit rapidly ripened by sudden exposure to the light. It is a fact that printing, the compass and gunpowder appeared on the scene at approximately the same time, when the fundamental sciences were flowering again after an eclipse of nearly fifteen centuries. But science's contribution to the inventions and discoveries was virtually nil. The compass was not born by applying the laws of electro-magnetism— quite the contrary. Descartes formulated the laws of optics long after Galileo built his first telescope and discovered the mountains of the moon, Jupiter's satellites and the phases of Mercury and Venus.

Newton's work is the most striking example of the gulf separating science and technology. Together with Einstein, he is undoubtedly the greatest scientific genius of modern times. His works have inspired three centuries in the knowledge of the laws of the universe, but it would be very hard to name a single practical application of his discoveries before the launching of the first sputnik. If the laws of gravity had remained unknown, nothing would have changed in the conquest of nature by man since the eighteenth century. Neither the steam engine (which was invented long before Nicolas Sadi Carnot formulated the theory behind it), nor electricity, nor chemistry owe anything to them.

That is rather disturbing if we think about it. The most creative inventors of modern times, those who have contributed most to changing the world, Denis Papin, Watt, Stephenson, Edison, Marconi, William G. Armstrong, Nicola Tesla and the brothers Lumière, were not what are commonly understood as "scholars". We could have lived as we live today on a quite different theoretical foundation, with a different conception of the universe, with unscientific, irrational or religious philosophies. After all, Nazism was an aberrant, magical philosophy and its technology almost conquered the world. After all, our rationalism and our materialism are also ideological choices rather than products of the spirit of truth. After all, evolutionism, on which our whole idea of progress rests, is a fairy-tale.

Something inside us revolts against such observations. We should like practical achievements to be rewards for what we hold to be our most noble desire: the desire for the truth. That is also why we want to deny that early men could have made any practical achievements, because they lived far removed from the truth. So when we discover central heating in ancient cities, our astonishment is tinged with anxiety. It is our mental world that totters. Small wooden forks that have emerged from pre-history jab at our minds. The bronze giant of Talos, on the shores of Crete, stones us. The builders of Stonehenge are hostile to us. Daedalus makes us begin to doubt ourselves. The Mayan calendar disturbs our mental constellations. And yet if we cannot help thinking of science and technology as inseparable, one look at nature should make us know better. There is not a single one of the useful inventions that have transformed our world that the animal world has not made before us. The squid and the insect called "stenos" propel themselves by jet-propulsion. Wasps make paper. The electric ray has fixed condensers, electric batteries and circuit breakers. Ants practice agriculture and stock-breeding, and they may even know the use of antibiotics. Near its head and tail, the fish *Gymnarchus niloticus* has tension generators and apparatuses capable of perceiving minute fluctuations in the electric field. The demon of "doing" is everywhere and circulates in a mysterious way through the whole of nature.

The fame of the astronomical science of the Babylonians continues to exist after three thousand years. In one sense, it is actually true that it went very far, farther than the Greeks did, and, in many fields, even farther than modern astronomy did up to the last century. Some twenty-five centuries ago, Kidinnu calculated the value of the annual movement of the sun and moon with an accuracy that was not surpassed until 1857, when Peter

Andreas Hansen, director of the Gotha observatory, obtained figures with no more than three seconds of arc of error. Kidinnu's figures had an error of less than nine seconds of arc.

Even more astonishing was the accuracy of Kidinnu's calculation of the eclipses of the moon. The present methods of calculation, established in 1887 by Theodor von Oppolzer, included an error of seventh-tenths of a second of arc in estimating the movement of the sun. Kidinnu's calculation was two-tenths of a second nearer the truth! Toulmin and Goodfield, who gave these figures in their lectures at Leeds University in 1957, made no secret of their admiration for the ancient Mesopotamian astronomer:

"It would seem incredible that such accuracy could have been achieved without watches, without the impressive mechanical apparatuses of our modern observatories and without higher mathematics, if we did not know that Kidinnu was able to consult astronomical archives extending over a much longer period than those available to his present-day successors."

Were Kidinnu and his colleagues great astronomers? No! Incredible as it may sound, their astronomical knowledge was practically nil! Surprising as it may seem, it was nowhere near the level of that of a modern schoolboy. Kidinnu and the other Babylonian "astronomers" believed that the planets were gods. They had absolutely no conception of the dimensions of the heavens and the mere idea of distance in space applied to the moon, the sun and the stars would have seemed just as absurd and scandalous as a trigometrical calculation of the movement of the angels or the distance between heaven and hell would seem to our modern theologians.

Strictly speaking, the astronomers who observed the movements of the planets for centuries from the top of their temple, the ziggurat, were theological engineers. The great ziggurat of Ur, whose colossal ruins still fill twentieth-century man with a sort of reverential awe, and rightly so, was not an observatory in any sense of the word. We should be nearer the truth if we imagined it as a gigantic vestry, with a study attached.

Incidentally, the Babylonian astronomical texts contained all the basic tenets on which Kidinnu's remarkable calculations were based. In the didactic poem *Enuma Elish,* which tells of the creation of the world by the supreme god, Marduk, it says: "Then Marduk created kingdoms for the great gods. He drew their image in the constellations. He established the year and its divisions, allotting three constellations for each of the twelve months.

"When he had defined the days of the year by the constellations, he ordered Nibiru (the lord of the Zodiac) to measure them all and in the center he fixed the zenith. He made Luna (the moon) the radiant mistress of the darkness and ordered her to inhabit the night and show the time. He ordained her disc to wax, month after month, without cease:

'At the beginning of the month . . . thou shalt shine for six days like a crescent, and like a semi-circle on the seventh day. At full moon, thou shalt be in opposition to the sun, in the middle of each month. When the sun shall overtake thee in the east on the horizon, thou shalt shrink and shalt form a crescent in reverse. . . And on the twenty-ninth day thou shalt be in line with the sun once again."

And so it continues, with the dispositions for the planets, the movements of the sun in the Zodiac, etc. Because of his invincible realistic illusions, modern man tends to interpret these texts as literary fictions intended to give a poetic description of facts, the material character of which would have been perfectly well known to the calculators on the Great Ziggurat. He cannot believe that such perfect calculations could have been made by men to whom the Moon, Venus, Mars and all the other stars were really gods. But there exists a perfectly explicit ancient text that leaves absolutely no doubt about the amazing ignorance of the Babylonian astronomers.

About 270 B.C., Berosos, whom we have already mentioned in connection with the Akpallus, emigrated to the island of Cos, in the Dodecanese, and there he taught the science of his country. His teachings were collected and 200 years later the Roman Vitruvius made a summary of them that has come down to us. To Berosos, heir of 2,000 years of Babylonian astronomy, the earth was flat, the sun moved above it at a constant altitude, and so did the moon, but a little lower down. The moon had a luminous side and a dark side and it revolved on itself in such an ingenious way that its monthly variations were explained, and yet so strangely that at the time of full moon it showed its dark side to the sun! Naturally Sun and Moon had to be gods, for after having disappeared every night and morning on the western horizon of a flat earth, they nevertheless reappeared the next day in the east by a miracle which only the great god Marduk could explain. But Berosos also dazzled the Greeks, who had known for a long time that the earth was round and what the main features of the celestial constellations were, by the fantastic precision of his ephemerides and his predictions of eclipses. The Greeks were scholars, Berosos was a technician. The practical work of the Babylonian astronomers required no theoretical knowledge and has left no trace of such knowledge.

The gap that separates science from technology becomes even more obvious when we remember that at the time when Berosos arrived on Cos, Aristarchus of Samos had already discovered that the earth rotates on its own axis, that it revolves round the sun once a year and that the last-named phenomenon implies the enormous dimensions to be attributed to space. But Aristarchus was not a technician and did not consider it his (in this case, theological) task to predict the eclipses to a tenth of a second of arc. He was satisfied to know how things happened and that appearances had been explained, as Plato put it.

In a sense, the intellectual adventure of the Greeks

illustrates the independent development of science and technology, for they, the first genuine scientists, always looked on technique as an attribute of slaves and barbarians, at least until Archimedes, the revolutionary genius who was both engineer and scholar. Admittedly, the Greeks were the first men in history to glimpse the true nature of the universe and its organization—the word "cosmos" which they have bequeathed to us, first meant beautiful, elegant, organized. Admittedly, they were the first to understand the predominant yet modest situation of man in the midst of this vast machine, yet practically none of the great inventions of their day were made by them. When Archimedes finally realized that the practical aspect of experimentation also formed part of true science, it was too late. As we know, he was murdered by a soldier of the victorious Roman army. With the Romans, technology once again replaced science.

We have quoted Vitruvius, whom the encyclopedias call an architect, because he used that designation himself. But in reality, the Roman architect was primarily an authentic engineer, like the Italian Renaissance architects.

The Roman architect, Sergius Orata, a contemporary of Julius Caesar, invented indirect central heating in the form which has recently become fashionable: under-floor heating. Until the end of the empire, Roman and Gallo-Roman engineers made a host of minor inventions which transformed everyday life (window panes, for example), without using any scientific knowledge at all. In the age of Augustus, schoolchildren still learned Euclid's geometrical theorems, but they were no longer taught the demonstrations. What was the point of learning them, since Euclid had already done it? This small detail shows better than anything else how far the Roman genius, so fertile in the art of transforming nature, was from the sources of scientific intelligence. If we walk alongside the remains of a great Roman aqueduct, for example, the one that supplied Carthage with water and crossed fifty miles of plains and hills, we are astounded by the accuracy of the calculations of gradient. But the men who made these calculations and the corresponding topographical measurements could no longer demonstrate the theorem of Pythagoras. Like our own modern engineers, like the engineers of ancient Babylonia, they had tables and abacuses to solve all the practical problems. But the scientific theory behind the tables was uninteresting and useless as far as they were concerned.

One of the strangest discoveries of modern archaeology, the significance of which Professor André Varignac was one of the first to emphasize, was that the fall of the Roman Empire was as much due to technical reasons as to political causes. When scholars opened the tombs of the barbarians that were erected over their remains as from the fifth century, they were surprised to find that their weapons were made of better steel than those of the Romans, and their armor, the harness of their horses and even of their chariots and carts were better, too. The wild Huns, whom we still think of with fear and trembling after so many centuries because of the evidence of the last Latin chroniclers, ultimately turn out to have brought with them inventions which no European people had any conception of, not even, indeed especially, the Greeks, although they were so good at unravelling the mysteries of the universe.

In fact, we are indebted to the Huns and Mongols for horseshoes, the rational harnessing of horses with a padded collar and even, indirectly, printing!

The long and complicated history of printing can be summed up as follows. At the beginning of the Christian era, the Chinese invented the art of wood engraving; the Mongols invaded China and India; in the latter country they learned how to play cards, the favorite distraction of soldiers at leisure. In order to renew their packs of cards, worn out by constant use, they used the Chinese technique of engraving, which they then spread as far as the gates of Europe. The western world adopted the invention and used it to make pious images, instead of playing cards. A Dutchman had the idea of separating the engraving that represented the image and that which told the legend into two parts, so that several images and several legends could be combined with one another by permutation. Then, once more in Holland and North Germany, the individual letters were separated from each other by yet other inventors. Lastly, in Mainz, Gutenberg invented the printing press, printers' ink and the use of metal alloys for letters.

If we think of these two inventions alone, modern saddlery and harnessing for horses and (indirectly) printing, we are forced to admit that what the Mongols brought with them to the west has done more to transform it than all the wonderful science of Greece, at least until the Renaissance. Yet the scientific background of printing and saddling with a horse-collar is non-existent. In the days of Rome's grandeur, geese, the rearing of which was a specialty in Great Britain, were exported to Italy in flocks. These flocks, driven by a series of constantly changing intermediaries, walked all through Gaul from Calais to the Alps in about a month. As soon as draught horses appeared, the same trade could be carried on in the form of patés and preserved goose. Transport was partly by barges, moving up and down the rivers, and partly by heavy chariots that played the same economic role as our modern railways. The draught horse opened up the countries north of the Danube and west of the Rhine so rapidly and extensively that they soon became as commercially important as the Mediterranean countries and even eclipsed them in the end. So civilization's ultimate conquest of northern Europe can be partly attributed to the Mongols. But who remembers that today, and what place do the Mongols occupy in the official history of progress?

Once we have got used to this idea, we find endless examples. Thus, there is no link between the abstract

Hellenist scientists of the second century B.C. and the engineers of Alexandria, who invented, among other things, the jet engine and the famous "ball of Heron," which Jean-Jacques Rousseau revived as a curiosity, two thousand years later.

The history of invention is boundless. The history of science is narrowly limited. Science is a river. Invention is an ocean. Science is mental conquest. Invention is the whole of nature herself at work in man. Science advances within the bounds of the possible. Invention is a blind victory over the impossible. In this sense, it is magic. But we are so alienated by ideology that we honestly believe that our modern concept of nature is the only valid one. And so our culture separates us from the dynamic reality of vanished worlds, just as our modern ideas about man separate us from the true depths and extent of the nature of man, from the dark regions where the spirit of creation moves past the spirit of reflection, where *doing,* completely indifferent to *knowing,* overtakes it.

If we link human genius with the power to create, then we associate it with freedom. In this sense, it is a modern expression and a modern conception. Our ancestors saw genius in the gods, or the memory of their great ancestors at work in man. And when we consider that most, if not all, of what we have achieved has been effected by nature working through living beings, are forced to admit that the genius of nature in man could have been given expression in many different ways during many vanished millennia. "We have the center of nature within us," said Paracelsus. "We are all in a state of creation. We are arable land." Creative power in its raw state, that which moves matter, that which shapes life, could have cultivated this arable land in many ways. The origin of man is constantly being backdated. New discoveries constantly reveal to us the existence of mysteriously advanced cultures in a past which only yesterday we imagine as inhabited by shaggy hirsute brutes banging two stones against each other in the dripping darkness of their caves.

If it is really true, as Marx thought, that discoveries are made when mankind needs them, what is the need which is met by these contemporary excavations which follow so closely on one another? Perhaps it is the need to feel that we are not alone, isolated in this adventure of the conquest of nature and of our human machine, that this adventure could have unfolded several times at various stages of fundamental knowledge, with similar successes and failures, with different conceptions of space and time. Perhaps, also the need to achieve a humanism useful for the future, to which we shall only accede through a re-humanization of vanished ages and with a general conception of the eternity of man.

# 2 The Twelve Cities of Catal Hüyük

We have mentioned many conjectural wonders in this book. For the benefit of those who prefer wonder with a solider base, we now introduce a culture, the existence of which is proved today. Four of its centers have already been identified. The most famous is called Catal Hüyük. James Mellaart was the man responsible for its excavation.

The chance find of an obsidian artifact in the south of Turkey excited Mellaart's curiosity. He thought that his find might have come from some unknown site on the edges of one of the volcanoes in Central Anatolia. The prospect of being able to establish the origin of the large numbers of weapons, tools and utensils made of the same material that had been excavated in several countries where there was no obsidian must have been enticing to an archaeologist. The localization of such a center of production would prove that as early as the Neolithic commercial relations had existed between Asia Minor, Mesopotamia, the Iranian plateau and probably various western countries, too. So the young scholar investigated the region of Konya. Two *tells* (Arabic for "hills") rose from the plain, thirty miles from the town and fifty from the volcano of Hassan Dagh.

Once Mellaart had begun to dig, the results surpassed his wildest hopes. He discovered twelve cities superimposed on each other, the most ancient of which must have been inhabited 9,000 years ago. With the exception of the last of the twelve cities, they had undoubtedly been destroyed by fire one after the other and rebuilt. Without even resorting to symbolism, the idea naturally comes to mind that these superimposed cities offer an analogy with our own civilization, which could equally well have been built on a pile of vanished cultures.

But what surprises us most at first is the degree of culture and the level of artistic and technical refinement postulated by the finds in these twelve cities.

Each city consisted of brick houses without doors. Access to the interior of the house was by a ladder leading to the roof/terrace. The total number of dwellings in each urban district was arranged like a bee's nest and formed a fortress offering protection against attacking enemies and the floods of the river Carsamba. The buildings had nearly all collapsed, but it was possible to reconstruct parts of the walls. It was found that they were covered with frescoes on the inside. However, the restorers came up against a difficulty. As soon as the colors were exposed to sunlight, they faded. Undoubtedly they were made from mineral pigments which deteriorated under the effect of light. The frescoes were rapidly photographed to keep a record of their original appearance. (Subsequently, various attempts were made to give them a protective covering in order to preserve the colors. Polyvinyl acetate gave satisfactory results.)

These murals represented various scenes. Hunting, games, ceremonies and people in different attitudes. The treatment is so realistic that we can read the dominant features of the people concerned: tremendous vitality and astute intelligence bordering on cunning. Their fashions in clothing were also reconstructed. The men wore woolen shirts, tunics and winter coats of leopard skin, with belts that had bone buckles. The hems of the women's dresses contained copper rings, like the brass rings which kept our grandmothers' crinolines stiff, to stop their skirts from riding up. The décolleté was rather daring. Jewels of lead, a very rare metal at the time, or copper inlaid with precious stones or carved hard stones completed their adornment. Nécessaires, which contained products with different shades, indicated that the use of make-up was not unknown. The beauties of Catal Hüyük had obsidian mirrors to check their appearance in. The sharp edges of the mirrors were covered with plaster so that they would not cut themselves.

Animals are also depicted in these frescoes: birds (mostly vultures), leopards and a great many bulls. Symbols also abound in these mural paintings: strange networks of intersecting red and black lines, rosettes, mandalas, two-edged axes (found again many thousands of years later among the Scythians, in Thrace and also in Crete), and quantities of crosses. But the commonest and most striking symbol depicted at Catal Hüyük is the human hand. We cannot help establishing a connection with the hands that Aurignacian men had already painted many tens of thousands of years earlier on the walls of their caves, for example, at Gargas in the Hautes Pyrénées, at Cabrerets in the Lot, and at Castillo near Santander. However, they had a different process, for they used a pad to apply the color round the hands, which were placed flat on the wall and then came out as negatives. In Catal Hüyük, the hands themselves were colored. Admittedly, we can only speculate about the significance they attached to the human hand. Could it be that man showed special consideration for this part of his body, on which according to the chiromancers of so many countries from Meso- potamia to China, the traits of his character and the principal events of his life were inscribed? Or should we see in the series of juxtaposed hands at Catal Hüyük a system of numbering, with each finger standing for a unit? But when the hands are pressed against the breasts, the symbol becomes clearer in the sense of a procreative invocation. . . .

If we consider all these symbols, plus the baked clay seals which have also been found in large numbers, we are astonished by the absence of any form of writing.

There were seals the size of a postage stamp in every house. They were used to mark ceramic objects and they were all different. This leads us to believe in the existence of strictly controlled private property and also of a social structure based on the family. The seals could be compared with our own coats of arms, but whereas the latter are the privilege of the nobility, the seals were present in every home. It has been suggested that these seals were used to sign messages written on perishable materials. But it is improbable that not the slightest trace of these materials has been preserved, even in a very different form, dust for example. Again, how can we explain that no inscriptions have been found on the frescoes so far brought to light? In view of their achievements in so many fields, it is difficult to imagine that the men of Catal Hüyük did not possess some written form of their language. Or is it simply that we cannot recognize this writing, or some subtle way of inscribing it? Perhaps we have to do with the heirs of the lost script of prehistory? Perhaps the writing was deliberately kept secret or forbidden? We can also ask whether they did not use invisible ink that only became visible after the application of a developer known to certain initiates.

Many sculptures and various religious objects were found in forty excavated sanctuaries. With their help, we can partially reconstruct the religion of the first citizens in the world (for that is what they are until the contrary is proved).

All the sanctuaries seem to have been dedicated to the Mother Goddess. The presence of this deity suggests that there was a link between all cultures in the dawn of mankind. Does not the image of the Mother Goddess also appear among the statuettes of the Solutrean era that were found at Willendorf in Austria, at Brassempouy in the Landes, in the Grimaldi cave at Menton and among the Tchouktchi Eskimoes? She is known by various names, Venus, Mother of Death, Mistress of the Earth, etc., depending on her multiple attributes, the main one of which is fecundity. Does not the shaman in Siberia address himself to the Mistress of the Earth, who in turn sends him to the Mistress of the Universe, for permission to use a lasso to catch the animals he depends on for his subsistence? Have not statuettes nearly 9,000 years old been excavated at Jarmo (Iraq)? Was she not worshipped at Eshmun in Mesopotamia, and at Baalbek? In Egypt she was identified with Maat, the goddess of right and truth; in Chaldaea, she is sometimes represented like a slender sylph, at others she is callipyginous. And is she not symbolized by the terra cotta figurines of mothers breastfeeding their children that were found at Tell Obeid? Scholars think they recognize her at Mohenjo Daro in the Indus valley, and as from the Vedic period she occupies a high place in the Indian pantheon. The Queen of Water in Mexico (water, the source of life) and the Fertility Goddess of the Minoans, fat at first, later slim, sometimes clothed and adorned, sometimes naked, are identified with her. In the Persian province of Luristan, we find various representations of her that are about 5,500 years old. And she is still present in Anatolia 4,000 years after the disappearance of Catal Hüyük. The links are missing, but we are tempted to rediscover her in the cult of Maya, the mother of Gautama Buddha and in the veneration of Mary, mother of Jesus. Is this Mother Goddess of the Universe a permanent presence?

In the statues found at Catal Hüyük, she is exclusively callipyginous. One of them shows her in the act of giving birth to a bull (a prefiguration of the Mithra cult?). Some mural paintings seem to imply that she can bring the dead to life again. Her color is red, the color of life; the color of death is black.

The frescoes contain pink, white, purple and (rarely) blue motifs, but strangely enough, never green ones. In some frescoes, it is possible to make out scenes relating to death; they seem to prove belief in a life hereafter. Corpses were stripped of their clothes and exposed to the mercy of the vultures on high places. There is obviously a comparison here with the adherents of Mazdaism. In the Achaemenid period, they still buried their dead, but after the reconquest of the empire by the Parthians, the custom of placing them on "towers of silence" spread and was adopted by the Parsees in India.

At Catal Hüyük, when only the skeleton was left, it was dressed in the dead man's clothes again and buried. A man's weapons and tools were placed in the tomb, as were a woman's jewels and various household implements, and children's toys. Fragments of cloth that were almost undamaged have been found in the tombs. They were all of excellent quality, especially the woolen cloths, which have helped us to distinguish three types of weaving. There were also cloths of goats' hair and felt. At present, they are the oldest textiles on our planet. We owe their preservation to two circumstances. Firstly, the fact that they did not come into contact with decomposing flesh, secondly the favorable moisture content of the air. But it may also be that the soil has special properties, like that of Isfahan. No soil analysis has yet been made at Catal Hüyük.

Among the normal objects that were buried with the dead man, some small wooden and bone forks are of exceptional interest. Such eating utensils are not found amount any other prehistoric people and the use of forks in the west was unknown until a few centuries ago. In addition to the forks, there were dishes of various sizes, plates, goblets, pitchers and cups of very delicate pottery.

So far, examination of the skeletons excavated has not enabled scholars to establish the dominant race. Various Mediterranean types, as well as Anatolians, have been found but digging continues and who knows what surprises are still in store for us. On the other hand, the ethnologists have been able to fix the approximate average age of thirty-two for men and thirty for women. This slight difference was presumably caused by too frequent pregnancies, as was formerly the case in India. Otherwise, women clearly held the first rank in this society.

One detail points to this, quite apart from the importance given to women in the religious sphere. Tombs were dug beneath the place which the beds of the deceased had occupied while they were alive. The men's beds were simple benches, whereas the mistress of the house was entitled to a very wide, almost majestic couch. Someday, perhaps, someone will establish a connection between all the different cultures scattered in time and space in which matriarchy was the norm: the predecessors of the Indo-Europeans in various regions of western Asia, certain Indonesian and Malaysian tribes, to quote only a few examples.

One would not be far wrong in assuming that the caste of priests and magicians, the wise men and technicians (though inferior in rank to the priestesses who alone were responsible for the ritual) knew how to make the most of the obsidian which was Catal Hüyük's main resource. There were three deposits of obsidian near the now extinct volcano. This material was used to make nearly all their weapons and tools: sickles, axes, scrapers for cleaning wool, points, various arms, lance- and arrowheads.

Now technically speaking, obsidian is a hard, black glass. Why should not the wise men of this city have tried to invent varieties of it with different colors and why should they not have been the first men to make glass, which we think should be attributed to the Phoenicians or the Romans?

And might not the expeditions of these technicians to the foot of the volcanoes of Hassan Dagh, Karaça Dagh and Mekke Dagh have given birth to the legend of Prometheus long before the Hellenic culture? To be sure, there is nothing on which to base this supposition, not even a legend, which born in that region of a real fact, was transmitted down the ages to the first generations of the historical era. The birth of the myth of Prometheus is not easily explicable by the geographical conditions in Greece and Crete. So why not seek its source around the craters of Central Anatolia which were active in those days?

Among the utensils found at Catal Hüyük, Mellaart was particularly struck by the mortars used to grind grain. Sometimes individual grains have left their imprints, or remained almost intact. And thanks to the genetic studies of the Danish professor Hans Halbart, the scholars had to admit that the inhabitants of the Neolithic city had not been content merely to gather ears of wild wheat; they actually cultivated three varieties of it. They also planted barley and lentils, and grew oleaginous and medicinal plants, almond trees and pistachio trees.

As we know, grains of wheat, the age of which can be established as approximately 10,000 years by the radio carbon method, have been found by American scholars in the caves of Mazanderan on the shores of the Caspian Sea. Not very long ago, in 1948, Robert J. Braidwood found millstones and ovens for baking bread during his excavations at Jarmo (Irak). These objects dated to 6750 B.C.

Mellaart thinks that these men, who had become shepherds and farmers, while still remaining hunters, must have realized the need to leave their houses that were scattered on the mountain slopes and live in communities on the plains, to make agriculture and stock-raising easier.

Thanks to the work of Maurits van Loot at Mureybat in north Syria, the scale of ages as far as agricultural communities is concerned has been pushed farther back. The communities discovered there came from the eighth millennium B.C., but nowadays we can no longer venture to establish a chronology with the dogmatism of the archaeologists and ethnologists of the past. Every year a new discovery in some part of the globe calls in question a culture's priority in time. The Syrian site excavated by van Loot lost its claim to be the oldest agricultural settlement after the recent discovery in Iran of the remains of a village dating back to 8500 years B.C. Perhaps others that are still more ancient will be found soon.

After a gap of several millennia, the second oldest site is Tell Hala, excavated by Oppenheim in 1911. It was inhabited between 3800 and 3500 B.C. But this overall picture, in which Uruk, the Hattites, Hittites and Hurrites succeeded each other, seems extremely precarious, in spite of its scientific precision.

What happened between the downfall of the last city of Catal Hüyük (about 5600 B.C.) and the expeditions the Sumerians made to buy copper (mentioned by Tashin Ozgüc, Director of the Archaeological Institute of Ankara University) in this region where so many events took place as from the beginning of the historical era? A region of which it was long believed that it had not even been organized into the most primitive kind of community in the Neolithic? As far as we know, the first commercial relations between Sumerians and Anatolians began more than twenty centuries after the mysterious disappearance of the last city excavated by Mellaart. How can we bridge this gap?

In a more recent period, the Assyrians set up an important trading post at Kanesh in the same region. It was on that site that Tashin Ogzüc and his colleagues excavated 14,000 engraved tablets. As yet no one has started to decipher them. Perhaps they might contain references to Catal Hüyük?

In 1967, Tashin Ogzüc found the remains of a town with a citadel and a necropolis at Altin Tepe. The site, which is in the east of present-day Turkey, once formed part of Urartu, which was built in the vicinity of Mount Ararat. Even before excavations had been undertaken in the territory of this vast empire, which collapsed in the sixth century B.C., we had a great deal of information about it from Assyrian texts. Still only a minor state in the second millennium, Urartu reached its apogee in the eighth century *B.C.*, not A.D. At that time, the Lydians looked on it as far more menacing and powerful than

Assyria. To the north it extended beyond the Caucasus, to the west, it crossed the Euphrates. In the east it had overthrown the Indo-Europeans of the region of Lake Urmiah. The most frequently quoted residence of their rulers, the exact position of which is not known even today, was Toprak Kaleh, on the shores of Lake Van. We do not know the origin of this people, but they were Asiatics, not Semites. We do not know what link existed between them and the citizens of Catal Hüyük, yet there are some striking similarities.

The discovery in 1939 and 1956 of the "Hill of Gold" (Altin Tepe) stimulated the Historical Foundation and the Turkish Government Department of Antiquities to carry out excavations. As a result, it was possible to reconstruct the everyday life, the technology, art and religion of the people. The walls of the precinct and the citadel were more than 30 ft. thick and the technique used in their construction shows great skill. A part of the already deciphered texts tells us something about the handling of blocks of granite weighing 40 tons, which the engineers raised to a height of 200 ft. and then fitted together. But even if the method is explained, it seems staggering that this feat was performed at Altin Tepe, just as, when confronted with the slabs at Baalbek, we ask where they came from and how they were transported and put in place.

Some texts referring to accounting and food stocks have also been deciphered. One of them tells us that 375,000 liters of wine were reserved for the use of the king and the nobility. Apart from the texts, certain objects provide valuable data. Motifs meticulously and artistically engraved on a gold disc suggest astonishing comparisons. Do we not see on it a god wearing a long robe and riding on a winged horse—an ancestor of similar gods in Greek mythology?

The tombs are small-scale replicas of the houses, as was later the case of the necropolis of Nagheh-e-Rustem. Here, too, the corpses were sumptuously dressed before burial. And as at Catal Hüyük, men's arms and women's jewels were placed in the stone or wooden coffins.

The luxury far exceeded that of other Neolithic cities. The furniture was decorated with gold and silver; the bronze legs of tables and beds were shaped like goats' feet or horses' hooves. Cauldrons were decorated with horses' heads. The artists had rulers and compasses to help them make the elaborate drawings for the frescoes.

However, all these fragments do not enable us to reconstruct a complete chain. Too many links are missing and the fact that the evidence is so widely scattered breeds multiple hypotheses. Although we know that Catal Hüyük disappeared when it was sacked in the middle of the sixth millennium, probably by the Scythians, we know nothing at all about its first foundation.

It is hard to believe that it was an experiment which turned out to be a masterpiece of urban planning and construction. Nor does the monopoly of obsidian adequately explain the origin of such a cultural center. Complicated techniques—for example, boring a hole finer than the thinnest needle in a block of hard stone—do not originate from nowhere. They presuppose many-sided talents. But was it not more probably a question of inheritance? It is scarcely credible that the culture of Catal Hüyük was the normal prolongation of the Upper Palaeolithic culture towards the end of the last ice age. And that applies equally to the civilization of priest technicians discovered recently in the Caucasus, in a region that certainly had contacts with the Neolithic city, for, as we have already mentioned, it had widespread commercial relations.

Was it really the first urban culture? How did it originate? Did it spring up suddenly? If not, what was its parentage? What was its heritage? Did it represent an advance on a past of which we know nothing, or was it the memory of some higher civilization?

Perhaps the inhabitants of Catal Hüyük themselves did

not know of or denied the existence of their predecessors, just as the inhabitants of Altin Tepe knew nothing of their forerunners. When their writing is finally deciphered, perhaps we shall read: "Only fools could claim that men as advanced as ourselves existed in the remote past."

# 3  The Empire of Daedalus

"I write in the age of Aries, for the age of Taurus has just past, and I speak to you over a span of more than three thousand years, to you who live at the moment of transition from Pisces to Aquarius. In your age, you have perfected many things that I began, and some of my technical achievements seem trivial and perhaps even puerile beside yours. Yet I have done things that no one before me did, and I created marvels that no one before me could create. My son and I have travelled through the sky where no man had even been, before us."

This is how Daedalus addresses in an imaginary message, with which Michael Ayrton begins his fine fictional autobiography of Daedalus.

The center of Daedalus's empire was Crete. There is much to support the view that it was probably the land which lives on in legend under the name of Atlantis.

There is no reliable information about Atlantis and many authors allot it another location. Plato placed it west of the Pillars of Hercules, i.e. west of the Straits of Gibraltar. With this in mind, people have sought for traces of Atlantis in the Atlantic. But in all probability the coastal inundations that took place in that region occurred slowly and gradually, more than 500,000 years ago. Yet the Greeks and Romans asserted that Atlantis disappeared suddenly. Solon heard about it during his stay in Egypt. The priests of Sais said that Atlantis was as big as Lydia and Asia together. That is certainly an exaggeration. In any case, the people of the Mediterranean littoral did not know the real dimensions of Asia at that time. In his *Critias*, Plato tells us of a war that broke out 900 years before his time between the rulers of Atlantis and the sovereigns of the Aegean Sea. According to his account, this would mean a kingdom that was considerably older than the Cretan empire. But as no single hypothesis has been confirmed or refuted so far, we can safely put forward other theories. This one, for example. A people who lived on an island in the Atlantic in the Neolithic could have transmitted the rudiments of their culture to the first Cretans, before their island disappeared, and we can easily imagine that one and the same catastrophe caused the downfall of Atlantis (regardless of its location) and the destruction of the Minoan culture on Crete.

A tremendous volcanic eruption could have eliminated one or more islands, whereas it might only have caused severe damage on the rest. In 1961, the Greek archaeologist Spiridon Marinatos found the remains of a city on the island of Thera (or Thira), the modern Santorin. It was established that it had been destroyed by the explosion of a subterranean volcano about 1500 B.C. In the scholar's opinion, it was only an episode in the history of the earth, which has unfolded very stormily in this part of the world. Santorin, which is 75 miles from Crete and 125 miles from Athens, is in the southern part of the Aegean. The catastrophe which struck it could also have affected other smaller islands in the same archipelago. According to the Greek seismologist Galanopoulos, the disaster probably began with earthquakes, followed by a tidal wave and two eruptions. Traces of lava dating to that century have been found all round the eastern Mediterranean and many papyruses mention that the sun grew dark in Egypt at the time. In 1902, when Mont Pelée on the island of Martinique re-erupted and the town of Saint-Pierre and the village of Morne-Rouge were destroyed by lava, red-hot ashes, torrents of boiling water and asphyxiating gases, the inhabitants of the neighboring island of Guadeloupe saw the sky grow dark in broad daylight because of the ashes in the sky. And among the debris of Saint-Pierre, people found the bodies of families sitting at table, of riders on horseback and workers at their jobs, just as in

Crete archaeologists excavated skeletons of men who had been surprised by the catastrophe when they were going about their everyday occupations.

Whatever the reason for the destruction of the Cretan cities, Galanopoulos is firmly convinced that they are identical with the cities of Atlantis: "Henceforth Atlantis and the Crete of Minos blend into the single image of a rich and powerful state, theoretically an ancient theocracy under a priest-king, but really a worldly and intelligent upper middle-class society, with a marked love of the theater and sport. The people dressed extremely elegantly, used ceramic utensils of great beauty and lived on terms of sexual equality (very rare in classical times)—all in all, a decadent, fascinating, delightful and doomed civilization . . ." Doomed? How and why?

Let us see what is known about this culture today. From many points of view, it borders on the marvelous.

Crete, as a sea power, dominated all the neighboring countries. There were constant commercial relations between the islands of the Cyclades and Asia from the Neolithic onwards. As it is probable that contacts existed between Central and Northern Asia, especially in the regions of the Caucasus and Turkestan and as it has also been shown that there were relations between these regions and Anatolia, they all had connection with Crete, too.

There were two phases in the era of expansions of the Cretans. In the first phase, they traded with Greece, Melos, Syros, Cyprus, Delos and Syria, and had cultural relations with Egypt. Their engineers, technicians and architects collaborated on the building of the pyramids of Senusert II and Amonemhat III. Even at this stage their fleet was a large one. It was to win for them the title of "Kings of the Sea." They also had a navy, the first such force in the northern Mediterranean, and they certainly reached Sicily and Spain.

It is quite likely that they did not subjugate the peoples they met there completely, but transmitted their own techniques generously, while profiting from these new contacts in their turn. Their power enabled them to perfect their arts and increase their prosperity by procuring the raw materials they lacked.

Copper was used at Tell Obeid as from the fourth millennium B.C. and in two books about Persia Herzfeld mentions axes of this metal that were found at Susa. Gold was already widely used and was considered to be the noblest of metals. There was gold in Asia, Africa and also in Europe. Its use was especially widespread in Ireland.

About 2400 B.C., tin made its appearance. It came from Saxony and Bohemia via the Adriatic; it came from Etruria via Sicily and lastly it was transported from Cornwall by way of Spain.

The use of iron, on the contrary, was very late everywhere—terrestrial iron, at least. In Egypt, they only began to exploit it towards 1400 B.C. A block of iron was found in a pyramid dating to 1600 B.C., but it had not been worked. Iron was not worked in Palestine until around 1200. The reason for this was that the many meteorites which undoubtedly landed in various parts of the world during the Neolithic (they are mentioned in all the traditions as rains of fire) contained iron in its pure state, so that it was unnecessary to extract it in the form of ore. As late as the twelfth century, Averroës, the Arabian philosopher and doctor, relates that a block of metal fell from the sky near Cordoba and that exceptional swords and sabres were made from it. According to the legend, Attila and, much later, Tamerlane owned their victories to the fact that their weapons were forged from a metal sent by god.

Their fleet enabled the Cretans to fetch tin from distant parts. They had workshops for treating bronze. Incidentally, bronze was not the only alloy that was used in protohistoric times. Other metals or metalloids were added empirically to copper—arsenic in Egypt, nickel in Germany, zinc in Saxony—to produce brass. Brass has also been found in the ruins of Kameiros, a town on

Rhodes. But the people who made it undoubtedly invented it by chance, for it is not found anywhere at that time in the optimum proportions.

If a little zinc or lead was added to bronze, a patina was obtained that was much sought after for use in the applied arts and sculpture. Moreover, an alloy of gold and silver called electrum was discovered at Ur. It was used later in the manufacture of coins. But one might ask whether the ancients did not sometimes confuse electrum, which had an unusual brilliance and tint, with aurichalcite (hydrozincile).

Classical authors frequently mention this substance. Many of them thought it was a pure, very rare metal. Others attributed a magic or divine origin to it. Plato praised the fiery sheen it gave to the objects and walls which were covered with it. A contemporary of Aristotle speaks of a shining white copper called mountain copper. The Mossynoeci (who undoubtedly lived in Asia Minor) obtained it, he said, by adding tin to copper and also a special earth from the shores of the Black Sea called calmia (hence the word "calamine"). Pliny the Elder also mentions this earth as being necessary for the manufacture of aurichalcite.

Their outstanding technical abilities enabled the Cretans not only to build splendid palaces, but also to fit them out internally in a way that no western people enjoyed until the nineteenth century A.D. Rooms arranged round a central courtyard. Double isothermic walls, covered on the inside with mosaics representing scenes from everyday life. Mosaics on the floor, some of which depict aquariums, the water in which seems to quiver so much owing to the movement of the aquatic plants, the bubbles and the darting fish that one hesitates to set foot on them for fear of falling in or disturbing the sleep of the lily-bedecked prince who presides statue-like over this charming scene that has been captured for eternity. But our delight turns to astonishment when we examine the sanitary installations. Drain pipes; air conditioning by a system of central heating, complemented in summer by the filtration of a permanent flow of cool air; a piped water supply; hydraulic lifts and subtle lighting in the living rooms and underground vaults. The arrangement of the passages in the palace and the whole street system of the city are equally carefully thought out. The buildings are separated from each other by alleys. In addition to living rooms, they include workshops, shops and sanctuaries. The roads, made of concrete or paved with flagstones, are barely 4 ft. 7 ins. wide. Some of them have two parallel U-shaped rails to act as gutters in stormy weather or perhaps also for the transport of ships "dry" from one harbor to another.

The Cretans founded towns like Akrotiri on all the islands of the Santorin group and perhaps in the Peloponnese, from the beginning of the second millennium onwards. Homer mentions that they had built a hundred on Crete itself. During the first phase, the urban area was on the east coast of the island. Then Cnossos in the north and Phaistos in the south moved it almost to the center of the island.

Towards 1750, a change took place, although its nature is not known. It may have been a revolution, invasion, or perhaps a natural catastrophe such as an earthquake or a tidal wave. A little later, new palaces were built, not only at Cnossos and Phaistos, but also at Hagia Triada and Tylissos. A certain rivalry seems to have existed between these two towns. They all went under about the middle of the fifteenth century B.C., except Cnossos, which lasted for another 50 years and then was wiped out, too.

The elegant women of Crete launched fashions which were imitated by the rich women of the neighboring islands, the towns of Asia Minor and Egypt. At first, they wore very long skirts with flounces; later they changed to fuller skirts without flounces. Their bodices were decorated with Medici-like collars; they were deeply cut at the front, leaving the breasts visible. Men were naked to the waist, wearing only a decorated loin-cloth or a smooth skirt, rather like those worn today by the Evzones, the soldiers of the Greek Royal Guard. Their dandyism was reflected in their headgear of flat turbans or tiaras. The women's hats would have rivaled those of the Parisiennes of la Belle Epoque in extravagance and variety. Incidentally, women seem to have enjoyed great freedom. We cannot deal in detail with all the aspects of Cretan social life, which can only be deduced from the pictorial evidence, since so far Cretan writing has only been partially deciphered.

The Cretan language comprises several written forms, one of which, linear B, seems to have been deciphered, although the work done on it by Ventris is controversial. Linear B would seem to indicate a date of about 1500 B.C. for the destruction of Cnossos. This shocks the archaeologists, but is apparently confirmed by geo-volcanic tests. Before linear B, there was linear A. What was there before linear A? We do not know. The lost writing?

No one has yet deciphered the famous disc of Phaistos, which probably dates to the beginning of the Minoan period. It was found in the palace of Phaistos, together with artifacts from the Middle Minoan period and a tablet with indecipherable inscriptions in linear A. The disc itself is of clay and bears ideograms and representations of objects. If it is contemporary with the objects, it dates to at least the seventeenth century B.C., but it may be even older.

Perhaps the excavations at Thera will provide new material for study. It is also possible that the writing on the disc of Phaistos is not a message, but a group of characters intended to be cut up and used separately.

Scholars have been able to reconstruct a great many details of the life and history of Crete, but some essential points are still obscure. When we consider myths and legends, the problem is that we do not possess data about the actual events which gave rise to them. For it is probable that all these myths that contain historical or technical data have a basis in reality. They have already provided us with a great deal of information. The researches of amateur archaeologists like Schliemann, who rediscovered Troy, or scholars like Victor Bérard, who reconstructed the *Odyssey*, were inspired by myths.

Among the subjects which remain obscure and puzzling, and susceptible of many interpretations, J. B. S. Haldane, who wrote about Daedalus, attributed an astonishing range of inventions to him: adhesives, contraceptives and artificial insemination. He is also reputed to have developed a machine for boring tunnels, a reverberatory furnace, a flying machine and a robot.

If we accepted these creations at their face value, they would, according to the myth, be the creation of a demigod, an improbable demi-god-cum-engineer, whose achievements would be even more wonderful than those of Hercules, for his twelve labors and adventures witness more to strength and willingness than to technical imagination.

What do we know about Daedalus? The son of Aries, the god of war, he was born at Athens. There he worked simultaneously in the fields of mechanics, architecture and sculpture, and made many innovations. His nephew and pupil was called Talos. Jealous of his skill, Daedalus threw him off the top of the Acropolis. Legend—or he himself—later gave the name of Talos to a giant robot he invented.

The gods had divided the earth up between them. Atlantis (i.e. Crete, according to our theory) fell to Poseidon. As from this phase, the multiple roles played by bulls in the myth are quite striking. God (Zeus in the opinion of many historians) assumed the shape of this animal to seduce the young maiden Europa. He swam with her to Crete and gave her three sons: Minos, Sarpedon and Rhadamanthus. Minos became king of the island and married Pasiphae. And she fell in love with a bull, just like Europa, her mother-in-law. At this moment, Daedalus was still working at the court of Minos. As he was a sculptor, he carved a cow out of wood. He hollowed out the carving. Pasiphae got inside it and so assuaged her passion with the bull. The son who was born of this amour had a man's body and a bull's head. It was the Minotaur. Minos ordered Daedalus to build him a labyrinth in which to hide this bastard, who shamed him in the eyes of the world.

The bull continues to play a decisive role in Cretan, and later, in Grecian mythology. It was because he had not sacrificed the bull that Poseidon made rise from the sea that Minos died. The seventh labor of Hercules consisted in taming a wild bull. Prometheus was chained because he gave Jupiter the fat and bones of a sacrificial bull to eat as a joke. We come across the bull again in Egypt and India. But what has all this got to do with Daedalus, the sculptor, mechanic, engineer and inventor?

We can interpret the myth in terms of depth psychology. We can also imagine Daedalus making genetic experiments, trying to produce hybrids with the animal-god, making attempts at artificial insemination. The people then composed a fabulous tale about it. Anyway, who was Daedalus? Just as there was not only one ruler called Minos, but a whole dynasty that bore the name, we can envisage a guild of Daedaluses. Generations of them, so to speak, belonging to some confraternity of investigators and technicians, whose work assumed a magical aspect to the uninitiated.

After the Argonauts had helped Jason to fetch the Golden Fleece, they wanted to land in Crete on the return journey. They were prevented by the intervention of a giant robot, called Talos, who protected the whole island by himself. He walked all round it three times a day. He detected foreign ships and threw rocks at them. But he had one weak point: his ankle. If he was wounded there, his vital fluid flowed out of it. Was the liquid from his tank? Did the machine invented by Daedalus run on naphtha (petroleum)? Petroleum was known to the ancients. We read in Theophrastus that certain peoples burnt stones, which gave off a vapor. When this vapor was led through pipes, it set machines in motion. The eternal fire lit by the Zoroastrian magi and before them, no doubt, by the priests of other fire-worshipping religions on the Iranian plateau and in the neighborhood of Mosul, was fed by natural gases escaping from the earth. From the most remote antiquity, it was the practice to collect "mumya," a sort of solidified bitumen with therapeutic and dynamic properties. The word "naphtha" does not figure in the texts that describe the robot Talos. We can imagine other sources of energy. We can also dream about this machine which detected the approach of ships and bombarded them with unerring aim. Medea, who favored the Argonauts, wounded Talos in the heel. The machine broke down . . . In the same way, the myth of Icarus flying is perhaps only the story of a technical experiment.

Naturally there is nothing to stop us from thinking that the Cretans and their Daedaluses owed the rudiment of science and technology to visitors who came from "outside," like the Akpallus. We can also imagine that the Cretans—especially the members of the Daedalus guild —were the guardians of the secrets of earlier highly developed cultures. The frescoes at Cnossos contain details showing a pair of "scales for weighing souls" and there are the remains of puzzling apparatuses in the palaces and workshops at Cnossos. Did the Daedaluses or their neighbors, playing at sorcerers' apprentices, try to harness volcanic energy and unintentionally blow up their world through their overweening ambition?

These questions are not absurd. Indeed it would be absurd not to put them, if we really believe in the permanent existence of an inventive intelligence in our history, which is still riddled with unexplored abysses.

When we have deciphered the unknown writings, when we have examined the myths, not with a patronizing and presumptuous attitude, but with minds open to the possibilities of earlier successes of the creative intelligence, open to the idea of the perpetual cycle of time (the past within the present and the present within the past), then at last there will be true humanity in human history.

# Bibliography

PART ONE: A Pleasure Trip in Eternity

1 Doubts about the Theory of Evolution

BERL, EMMANUEL, "L'évolution de l'évolution," in *Preuves*, Nos. 166 and 167. December 1964–January 1965.

BOUTHOUL, GASTON, *Variations et mutations sociales*, Payot, Paris, 1969.

CUENOT, LUCIEN, *L'Évolution biologique. Les faits, les incertitudes*, Masson, Paris, 1951.

DEWAR, D., *The Transformist Illusion*, Dehoff Publications, Murfreesboro, Tennessee, 1957.

DOBZHANSKY, THEODOSIUS, *Evolution, Genetics and Man*, Chapman & Hall, London, 1955.

EDWARDS, FRANK, *Strange World*, Lyle Stuart, New York, 1964.

ENGEMANN, JOSEPH G., "Pogonophora, The Oldest Living Animals?," in *Papers of the Michigan Academy of Science, Arts and Letters*, Vol. LIII, 1968.

LEACH, GERALD, "Oldest Skull Found," in *The Observer*, 17.8.1969.

LE GROS CLARK, W. E. and LEAKEY, L. S. B., "The Miocene Homonoidea of East Africa," in *Fossil Mammals of Africa*, British museum: H.M.S.O., London, 1951.

LEWIS GAZIN, C., "A Review of the Middle and Upper Eocene Primates of North America," in *Smithsonian Miscellaneous Collections*, Vol. CXXXVI, No. 1, July 1958, pp. 1–112.

MAN, OLDER, "Longer Pleistocene," in *Scientific American*, February 1963.

RODDAM, JOHN, *The Changing Mind*, Jonathan Cape, London, 1967.

ROSENFELD, ALBERT, *The Second Genesis: The Coming Control of Life*, Prentice-Hall, New York, 1969.

SCHIRMBECK, HEINRICH, *Ihr werdet sein wie Götter. Der Mensch in der biologischen Revolution*, Diederichs, Düsseldorf, 1966.

SIMONS, ELWYN L., "A Critical Reappraisal of Tertiary Primates," in *Evolutionary and Genetic Biology of Primates*, Vol. I, ed. J.-B. Janusch, Academic Press, London, 1963.

—— "Some Fallacies in the Study of Hominid Phylogeny," in *Science*, Vol. CXLI, September 1963, pp. 879–89.

VANDEL, ALBERT, *La Genèse du vivant*, Masson, Paris, 1968.

VANDERMEERSCH, BERNARD, "Les origines de l'homme," in *Atomes*, No. 272, January 1970.

## 2   Continental Drift

BABCOCK, WILLIAM H., *Legendary Islands of the Atlantic (American Geographical Society Research Series*, No. 8), New York, 1922.

GIRAUD, JACQUELINE, "Quand l'Afrique était au pôle Sud," in *L'Express*, 25/31.5.1970.

HAPGOOD, CHARLES H., *Earth's Shifting Crust*, Museum Press, London, 1959.

—— *Maps of the Ancient Sea Kings. Evidence of Advanced Civilization in the Ice Age*, Chilton Co., Philadelphia, 1966.

HURLEY, P. M., *How Old is the Earth?*, Heinemann Educational, London, 1960.

PELTANT, SARAH, "La dérive des continents," in *Planète*, No. 35, July 1967 (summary of an article in *Science and Technology*).

REBEYROL, YVONNE, "A la recherche du Gondwana," in *Le Monde*, 18.12.1969.

DE CAMP, LYON SPRAGUE, and LEY, WILLY, *Lost Conti-*

*nents. The Atlantis Theme in History, Science and Literature,* Gnome Press, New York, 1954.

## 3 The History of the "Impossible Maps"

This chapter is a reproduction of an article by Paul-Émile Victor in the review *Planète*, No. 29, July 1966, entitled "L'énigme Piri Reis."

## 4 The Earth's Scars

ANDERS, E., "Origin, Age and Composition of Meteorites," in *Space Science Review*, No. 3, 1964, p. 583.

AXON, M. J., "Metallurgy of Meteorites," in *Progress in Material Science*, No. 13, 1963, p. 183.

ENEVER, J. E., "Giant Meteor Impact," in the anthology *Analog 6*, Pocket Books, New York, 1968.

SULLIVAN, WALTER, *We Are Not Alone*, McGraw-Hill, New York, 1966.

WOOD, JOHN A., *Meteorites and the Origin of Planets*, McGraw-Hill, New York, 1968.

## 5 Two Fairy-tales Throw Light on the Earth's History

BAKER, GEORGE, "Tektites," in *Memoirs of the National Museum of Victoria*, No. 23, Melbourne, 1.7.1959, pp. 1–313.

BARNES, VIRGIL E., "North American Tektites," in *The University of Texas Publications*, June 1940, pp. 447–582.

CALDWELL, R., "Tal-i-Iblis et les débuts de la métallurgie due cuivre," in *Archéologie vivante*, No. 1, September 1968.

DALY KING, G., *The States of Human Consciousness*, University Books, New York.

DIOP, CHEIKH ANTA, *Antériorité des civilisations nègres*, Presence Africaine, Paris, 1967.

GARDNER, MARTIN, *Les magiciens démasqués*, Presses de la Cité, Paris, 1967.

GOLEYT, NOLEYM, *La Pyramide perdue*, Moscow, 1965.

O'KEEFE, JOHN A., *Tektites*, The University of Chicago Press, London, 1963.

RICHMOND, WALT and LEIGH, *The Lost Millennium*, Ace Books, New York.

VELINKOVSKY, IMMANUEL, *Worlds in Collision*, Victor Gollancz, London, 1950.

VIDAL, JEAN, "Medzamor ou le plus vieux complexe industriel du monde," in *Science et Vie*, July 1969.

WORSLEY, PETER, *The Trumpet Shall Sound: A Study of "Cargo" Cults in Melanesia*, MacGibbon & Kee, London, 1967.

PART TWO: Reveries about the Great Language

## 1 The Music of the Giants' Ballet

ARLETT, DOMINIQUE, "Stonehenge décodé," in *Planète*, No. 38, June 1968.

BROMAGE, BERNARD, *The Occult Arts of Ancient Egypt*, Aquarian Press, London, 1960.

DE CAMP, LYON SPRAGUE and CATHERINE, *Ancient Ruins and Archaeology*, Souvenir Press, London, 1963.

HAWKINS, GERALD S., *Stonehenge Decoded*, Souvenir Press, London, 1966.

JOYAUX, JULIA, *Le langage, cet inconnu*, Denoël, Paris, 1969.

MOYEIKO, IGOR, *Drugie 27 Tchuda*, Moscow, 1969.

NIEL, FERNAND, *Dolmens et menhirs*, Presses universitaires, Paris, 1958.

ROCHE, DENIS, *Carnac. Le mégalithisme. Archéologie, typologie, histoire, mythologie*, Hachette, Paris, 1969,

SAINT-BLANQUAT, HENRI DE, "Le Secret des menhirs corses," in *Sciences et Avenir*, No. 269, July 1969, p. 584.

## 2 The Hundredth Name of the Lord

BORGES, JORGE LUIS, *Sämtliche Erzählungen*, Munich, 1970.

CHIERA, EDWARD, *They Wrote in Clay*, University of Chicago Press, London & Chicago, 1935.

DEUEL, LEO, *The Treasures of Time*, Souvenir Press, London, 1966.

FRAZER, JAMES GEORGE, *The Golden Bough*, Macmillan & Co., London, 1890.

FULCANELLI, *Le Mystère des cathédrales*, Jean Schemil, Paris, 1926 and Pauvert, Paris, 1964.

GORDON, CYRUS H., *Before the Bible. The Common Background of Greek and Hebrew Civilizations*, Collins, London, 1962.

HARDEN, DONALD, *The Phoenicians*, Thames & Hudson, London, 1962.

HUTCHINSON, R. W., *Prehistoric Crete*, Penguin Books, Harmondsworth, 1962.

JOYAUX, JULIA, *La langage, cet inconnu*, Denoël, Paris, 1969.

KAHN, DAVID, *The Code-Breakers*, Weidenfeld & Nicolson, London, 1968.

LEROI-GOURHAN, ANDRÉ, *Les Religions de la préhistoire*, Presses universitaires, Paris, 1964.

MORFILL, W. R., *The Book of the Secrets of Enoch*, Clarendon Press, Oxford, 1896.

MOSCATO, SABATINO, *The Face of the Ancient Orient*, Routledge & Kegan Paul, London, 1960.

ROHMER, SAX, *The Romance of Sorcery*, Methuen & Co., London, 1914.

## 3 In Search of a Language of the Absolute

BORGES, JORGE LUIS, *Das Eine und Vielen. Essays zur Literatur*, Munich, 1966.

CADE, C. MAXWELL, *Other Worlds than Ours*, Museum Press, London, 1966.

FORBES, R. J. and DIJKSTERHUIS, E. J., *A History of Science and Technology*, Penguin Books, Harmondsworth, 1968.

FREUDENTHAL, HANS, *Lincos. Design of a Language for Cosmic Intercourse*, North-Holland Publishing Co., Amsterdam, 1960.

HOGBEN, LANCELOT, "Astraglossa or First Step in Celestial Syntax," in *Journal of British Interplanetary Society*, No. 2, 1959, p. 258.

HOYLE, FRED, *Of Men and Galaxies*, Heinemann, London, 1965.

LASZLO, ERVIN, "The Recovery of Intuitive Wisdom in Contemporary Science," in *Main Currents*, Vol. XXV, No. 5, May–June, 1969.

REISER, OLIVER L., "The Role of Symbols in Human Experience," in *Main Currents*, Vol. XXV, No. 5, May–June, 1969.

PART THREE: The Greatest Question of All

1 The Mysterious Akpallus

DRAKE, WALTER, *Spacemen in the Ancient East*, London, 1968.

FIRSOFF, VALDEMAR A., *Life Beyond the Earth. A Study in Exobiology*, Hutchinson, London, 1963.

KRASOVSKI, "Astronauts and Extraterrestrial Civilizations," in *Izvestia*, 4.5.1961. (In Russian.)

SCHNABEL, PAUL, *Berossos und die babylonisch-hellenistische Literatur*, Taubner, Leipzig, 1923.

SHKLOVSKI, JOSIF C., and SAGAN, CARL, *Intelligent Life in the Universe*, Holden-Day, San Francisco, 1966.

PART FOUR: About the Right to Ask Questions

1 Pocket Guide for Lovers of Historical Puzzles

BIRKET-SMITH, KAJ, *The Paths of Culture*, University of Wisconsin Press, Madison, 1965.

DEWAR, JAMES, *The Unlocked Secret*, William Kimber, London, 1966.

HOLE, FRANK, and HEIZER, ROBERT F., *An Introduction to Prehistoric Archaeology*, Holt, Rinehart & Winston, London, 1965.

JACOBS, MELVILLE, *The Anthropologist Looks at Myth*, University of Texas Press, London, 1966.

KOSAMBI, D. D., *Culture and Civilization of Ancient India in Outline*, Routledge & Kegan Paul, London, 1965.

MCGARRY, TERENCE, "Tracking Snake God to Origins," in *International Herald Tribune*, 4.9.1969.

MASON, J. ALDEN, *The Ancient Civilizations of Peru*, Penguin Books, Harmondsworth, 1957.

MÉTRAUX, ALFRED, *The Incas*, Studio Vista, London, 1965.
—— *Religions et magies indiennes d' Amérique du Sud*, Gallimard, Paris, 1967.

PRICE, DEREK JOHN DE SOLLA, *Science since Babylon*, Yale U.P., London, 1962.

RUZO, DANIEL, *La Cultura "Masma,"* Lima, 1954.

SEABROOK, WILLIAM, *Witchcraft*, G. G. Harrap, London, 1941.

HANSEN, L. TAYLOR, *He Walked the Americas*, Neville Spearman, London, 1963.

2   The Statistician in the Stone-Age Cave

This chapter is based on an article by Aimé Michel, "Revolution en préhistoire," in *Planète*, No. 28, May–June, 1966.

LEROI-GOURHAN, ANDRÉ, *Originalité biologique de l'homme*, Paris, 1957.
——*Les Religions de la Préhistoire*, Presses universitaires, Paris, 1964.

3   The Unknown Men of Australia

BORDES, FRANÇOIS, *Le Paléolithique dans le monde*, Hachette, Paris, 1968.

CLIFTON, TONY, "The Savage Awakening," in *The Sunday Times*, 7.12.1969.

MULVANEY, D. J., "The Prehistory of the Australian Aborigine," in *Scientific American*, March, 1966.

## 4 Communication between the Worlds

ASIMOV, ISAAC, *Is Anyone There?*, Rapp & Whiting, London, 1968.

DE CAMP, LYON SPRAGUE and CATHERINE, *Ancient Ruins and Archaeology*, Souvenir Press, London, 1965.

FAWCETT, Colonel P. H., *Exploration Fawcett*, Hutchinson, London, 1953.

HEYERDAHL, THOR, *American Indians in the Pacific*, Allen & Unwin, London, 1952.

HOMET, MARCEL F., *On the Trail of the Sun Gods*, Neville Spearman, London, 1965.

VERRILL, ALPHEUS HYATT and RUTH, *America's Ancient Civilizations*, G. P. Putnam's Sons, New York, 1953.

WAERDEN, BARTEL L. VAN DER, *Science Awakening*, P. Noorhoff, Groningen, 1954.

WILKINS, HAROLD T., *Mysteries of Ancient South America*, Rider & Co., London, 1946.

## 5 About Ancient Chinese Science

*I-Ging. Das Buch der Wandlungen*, Zurich, 1949.

JUNG, C. G., Psychology and Religion: West and East, Complete Works Vol. 11, Routledge & Kegan Paul, London, 1958.

NEEDHAM, JOSEPH, *Clerks and Craftsmen in China and the West*, Cambridge University Press, London, 1970.

—— *The Development of Iron and Steel Technology in China*, Newcomen Soc., London, 1958.

—— *The Grand Tritration*, Allen & Unwin, London, 1969.

—— *Science and Civilization in China*, Vol. I, Cambridge University Press, London, 1954.

—— *Science and Technology in China*, Oxford.

—— and DOROTHY, *Science Outpost* (*Papers of the Sino-British Science Co-operation Office*), *1942–1946*, Pilot Press, London, 1948.

PARETI, LUIGI and others. *The Ancient World*, 3 vols., Allen & Unwin, London, 1965. (UNESCO History of Mankind.)

## 6  A Trip round Numinor

BERGOUNIOUX, FRÉDÉRIC MARIE, and GLORY, A., *Les Premiers hommes*, Didier, Paris, 1952.

BOULE, MARCELLIN, *La Préhistoire*, Paris, 1928.

BREASTED, JAMES HENRY, *The Conquest of Civilization*, Harper & Bros., New York and London, 1926.

CARRINGTON, DOROTHY, *Découvertes archéologiques de Filitosa en Corse.*

LENGYEL, LANCELOT, *Le secret des Celtes*, Weber, Paris, 1969.

LOT-FALCK, EVELINE, *Les Chamans et les Maîtres de la Vie.*

MALLET, P. H., *Edda ou Monuments de la mythologie et de la poésie des anciens peuples du Nord*, Barde, Geneva.

MARKALE, JEAN, *Les Celtes*, Payot, Paris, 1969.

MOORET, ALEXANDRE and DAVY, G., *Des Clans aux empires. L'organisation sociale chez les primitifs et dans l'orient ancient*, Paris, 1923.

MORGAN, JACQUES DE, *L'Humanité préhistorique*, Paris, 1921.

OXENSTIERNA, ERIC, *The Norsemen*, Studio Vista, London, 1966.

PITTARD, EUGÈNE, *Race and History*, Kegan Paul, London, 1926.

RICKARD, T. A., *Man and Metals*, McGraw-Hill Book Co., London, 1932.

VENDRYES, JOSEPH, *Language*, Kegan Paul, London, 1925.

PART FIVE: About some Wonderful Semi-Certainties

## 1 The Free Union of Knowing and Doing

BERGIER, JACQUES, "La Technique comme société secrète," lecture at the Odeon Theatre of France, 19.2.1963.

DE CAMP, LYON SPRAGUE, *The Ancient Engineers*, Souvenir Press, London, 1969.

GOODFIELD, JUNE and TOULMIN, STEPHEN, *The Ancestry of Science*, 3 vols., Hutchinson, London, 1961–65.

MICHEL, AIMÉ, "Les ingénieurs de l'antiquité," in *Planète*, No. 12, September, 1963.

VARAGNAC, ANDRÉ, *De la préhistoire au monde moderne. Essai d'une anthropodynamique*, Plon, Paris, 1954.

## 2 The Twelve Cities of Catal Hüyük

BEEK, GUS VAN, "South Arabian History and Archaeology," in *The Bible and the Ancient Near East*, ed. G. Ernest Wright, Routledge & Kegan Paul, London, 1961.

—— *Hajar Bin Humeid. Investigation at a Pre-Islamic Site in South Arabia*, John Hopkins Press, London, 1969.

BOWEN, RICHARD LeBARON, Jr., and ALBRIGHT, FRANK P., *Archaeological Discoveries in South Arabia*, Johns Hopkins Press, London, 1958.

BRAIDWOOD, ROBERT J., *Jericho and the Setting of Near-Eastern History*, Chicago, 1957.

—— and HOWE, BRUCE, *The Late Prehistorical Sequence along the Hill Flanks of the Taurus and the Zagros*.

CARRINGTON, DOROTHY, *Découvertes archéologiques de Filitosa en Corse*.

GLEB, IGNACE J., "Inscriptions from Alishar and Vicinity," in *Oriental Institute Publications*, Vol. XXVII, Chicago, 1935.

GHIRSHMAN, ROMAN, *Iran: From the Earliest Times to the Islamic Conquest*, Penguin Books Harmondsworth, 1954.

GLOTZ, GUSTAVE, *L'histoire grecque*, Vol. I: *Des Origines aux guerres médiques*, Paris, 1925.

GODARD, ANDRÉ, *The Art of Iran*, Allen & Unwin, London, 1965.

—— *Le Trésor de Ziwiyé* (*Kurdistan*), Haarlem, 1950.

LEWY, JULIUS, "Some Aspects of Commercial Life in Assyria and Asia Minor in the Nineteenth Pre-Christian Century," in *Journal of the American Oriental Society*, Vol. LXXVIII, No. 2, June 1958, pp. 89–101.

LLOYD, SETON, *Early Anatolia. The Archaeology of Asia Minor before the Greeks*, Penguin Books, Harmondsworth, 1956.

LOT-FALCK, EVELINE, *Les Chamans et les Maîtres de la vie.*

MELLAART, JAMES, *Çatal Hüyük*. Thames & Hudson, London, 1967.

MORGAN, JACQUES DE, *L'Humanité préhistorique*, Paris, 1921.

OUSELEY, SIR WILLIAM, *Travels in Various Countries in the East*, Vol. 2, Rodwell, London, 1830.

OZGÜC, TASHIN, Altintepe, Ankara, 1966/9. (Turkish-English.)

—— "Ancient Orient," in *Scientific American*, March 1967.

—— "New Finds in the 'Karum' of Kanesh," in *The Illustrated London News*, 6.10.1961.

—— "Where the Assyrians Built a Commercial Empire in Second Millennium Anatolia: Excavating the 'Karum' of Kanesh," in *The Illustrated London News*, 14.1.1950.

VIDAL, JEAN, "Catal Hüyük," in *Science et vie*, May 1968, pp. 80–88.

3   The Empire of Daedalus

BERGOUNIOUX, FRÉDÉRIC MARIE and GLORY, A., *Les Premiers hommes*, Didier, Paris, 1952.

BREASTED, JAMES HENRY, *The Conquest of Civilization*, Harper & Bros., New York and London, 1926.

CAVAIGNAC, EUGÈNE, *Histoire du monde*, Vol. III, De Boccard, Paris, 1936.

CHAMBRUN-RUSPOLI, MARTHE DE, *L'Epervier divin*, Mont-Blanc.

DE CAMP, LYON SPRAGUE, *The Ancient Engineers*, Souvenir Press, London, 1969.

DEVIGNE, ROGER, *L'Atlantide*, Paris, 1924.

EVANS, ARTHUR, *The Palace of Minos*, 4 vols., Macmillan & Co., London, 1921–36.

FABRICIUS, ERNST, "Altertümer auf der Insel Samos," in *Mitteilungen des Deutschen Archäologischen Institutes in Athen*, Vol. IK, Athens, 1884, pp. 163–197.

GALANOPOULOS, A. G. and BACON, EDWARD, *Atlantis*, Nelson, London, 1969.

GERNET, LOUIS and BOULANGER, ANDRÉ, *Le Génie grec dans la religion*, Paris, 1932.

GLOTZ, GUSTAVE, *L'Histoire grecque*, Vol I, *Des Origines aux guerres médiques*, Paris, 1925.

HALDANE, J. B. S., *Daedalus; or, Science and the Future*, Kegan Paul, London, 1924.

HERZFELD, ERNST, *Iran in the Ancient East*, O.U.P., London, 1941.

MAULNIER, THIERRY, "La Cité ensevelie d'Akroliripar," in *Le Figaro*, 15.10.1969.

PRICE, DEREK JOHN DE SOLLA, "Ancient Greek Computer," in *Scientific American*, June 1959.

REY, ABEL, *La Science orientale avant les Grecs*, La Renaissance du livre, Paris, 1942.

RICKARD, T. A., *Man and Metals*, McGraw-Hill Book Co., London, 1932.

TOUTAIN, JULES, *The Economic Life of the Ancient World*, Kegan Paul, London, 1930.

VENDRYES, JOSEPH, *Language*, Kegan Paul, London, 1926.

WILLETTS, RONALD F., *Ancient Crete. A Social History*, Routledge & Kegan Paul, London, 1965.

WILLIAMSON, J., *The Reign of Wizardry*, Lancer Books, New York.

# AVON ◆ NEW LEADER IN
# WITCHCRAFT AND THE OCCULT

**THE DEVIL'S MARCHIONESS**
William Fifield                                    10165    $1.25

**FIFTY YEARS A MEDIUM**
Estelle Roberts                                    07286      .95

**THE GIRL FROM YESTERDAY**
Sarah Hughart                                      03228      .75

**THE HIDDEN SPECTRE**
Robert Tralins (Editor)                            01180      .60

**THE INFERNAL IDOL**
Henry Seymour                                      01107      .60

**MORNING OF THE MAGICIANS**
Louis Pauwels and Jacques Bergier                  15768     1.50

**THE SATANIC BIBLE**                              05389      .95

**THE SATANIC RITUALS**
Anton Szandor LaVey                                10629     1.25

**A WALK WITH THE BEASTS**
Charles M. Collins (Editor)                        01081      .60

---

Available wherever paperbacks are sold, or directly
from the publisher. Include 15¢ per copy for mailing;
allow three weeks for delivery.

Avon Books, Mail Order Dept.
250 West 55th Street, New York, N.Y. 10019

# THE BIG BESTSELLERS
# ARE AVON BOOKS!

*I'm OK—You're OK*
Thomas A. Harris, M.D.     14662    $1.95

*Jonathan Livingston Seagull*
Richard Bach     14316    $1.50

*Open Marriage*
Nena O'Neill and George
O'Neill     14084    $1.95

*Memo from David O. Selznick*
Rudy Behlmer     15412    $1.95

*The Eiger Sanction*
Trevanian     15404    $1.75

*The Brothers System for Liberated
Love and Marriage*
Dr. Joyce Brothers     15834    $1.50

*Island Paradise*
P. R. Pickney     15388    $1.50

*I Come As a Thief*
Louis Auchincloss     15438    $1.50

*Signs and Portents*
Al Hine     14845    $1.25

*Don't Embarrass the Bureau*
Bernard F. Conners     14852    $1.50

*The Ancient of Days*
Irving A. Greenfield     14860    $1.60

*Ringolevio*
Emmett Grogan     14449    $1.50

*The Barracudas*
Keefe Brasselle     14639    $1.50

*Net Net*
Isadore Barmash     14621    $1.50

---

Where better paperbacks are sold, or directly from the
publisher, include 15¢ per copy for mailing; allow three
weeks for delivery.

Avon Books, Mail Order Dept.
250 West 55th Street, New York, N. Y. 10019